Race, Class, and Culture

SUNY Series in Afro-American Studies

John Howard and Robert C. Smith, editors

Race, Class, and Culture

A Study in Afro-American Mass Opinion

Robert C. Smith
and
Richard Seltzer

State University of New York Press

A Portion of chapter 1 appeared in a different form in Robert C. Smith, "Sources of Urban Ethnic Politics: A Comparison of Alternative Explanations." In *Research On Race and Ethnic Relations,* Vol. 5, edited by Cora Bagley Marrett and Cheryl Leggon (Greenwich, CT: JAI Press, 1988): 159–91.

Published by
State University of New York Press, Albany

For information, address State University of New York
Press, State University Plaza, Albany, N.Y. 12246

Production by Dana Foote
Marketing by Fran Keneston

Library of Congress Cataloging-in-Publication Data

Smith, Robert Charles, 1947–
      Race, class, and culture : a study in Afro-American mass opinion /
by Robert C. Smith and Richard Seltzer.
          p.   cm. — (SUNY series in Afro-American studies)
      Includes bibliographical references and index.
      ISBN 0–7914-0945–7 (acid-free). — ISBN 0–7914-0946–5 (pbk. : acid
-free)
          1. Afro-Americans—Attitudes. 2. Afro-Americans—Politics and
government. 3. Public opinion—United States. 4. Political
culture—United States. 5. United States—Politics and
government—1989– I. Seltzer, Richard, Ph. D. II. Title.
III. Series.
      E185.615.S582   1992
      305' .896'073—dc20
                                                                                  91–8824
                                                                                    CIP

10 9 8 7 6 5 4 3 2 1

Contents

Tables

Preface

Not since Marx's 1967 study has there been a comprehensive book-length work on national level Afro-American mass opinion. Much has occurred since then in the configuration of America's race problem. Mass protests, violent rebellions in the ghettos and militant political leadership and organization have withered away. Afro-American politics is increasingly institutionalized in elections and related forms of systemic political participation. The "white backlash" and the conservative reaction represented by the political campaigns of George Wallace have been institutionalized in the administrations of Richard Nixon, Ronald Reagan, and George Bush. Afro-American society is increasingly bifurcated between a relatively secure and prosperous middle class and an underclass characterized by poverty and dispossession. In the last several years an articulate, outspoken, well-funded black conservative leadership group has emerged, and Jesse Jackson has twice sought the Democratic presidential nomination as a left-liberal progressive, winning overwhelming Afro-American mass support but relatively little support from white voters. Thus, a new, comprehensive study of Afro-American mass opinion is long overdue. Marx's study, for example, was largely concerned with understanding the sources and strength of black militancy and nationalism in mass society. The important changes in Afro-American society and politics observed in the last 20 years suggest interesting new questions for students of race in the United States.

One of these questions has been explored in detail in recent years. It deals with the effect on mass opinion of the increasingly sharp socioeconomic divisions in the black community; specifically, on whether conservatism is finding increasing support in the new black middle and upper classes (Bolce and Gray, 1979; Dillingham, 1981; Welch and Combs, 1983, 1985; Parant and Stekler, 1985; Seltzer and Smith, 1985b; Welch and Foster, 1986; Gilliam, 1986; Tate, 1986; Gilliam and Whitby, 1989). Although there is a substantial literature on this question, the evidence remains fragmentary, noncumulative, and inconclusive. A major reason is that a number of the studies are based on surveys that include insufficient numbers of blacks to permit detailed intraracial class analysis, a problem that characterizes much of the extant literature on Afro-American political culture, mass opinion, and voter behavior (see Walton, 1985: chaps. 2–5 for a discussion of the problem). Another problem of this literature is the absence of any theoretical frame of reference; rather, most students begin with the assumption of Welch and Foster that "If the black middle class were no different in its political beliefs than the black lower classes, they would indeed be an exception in American society" (1986:4). This formulation, of course, ignores the well-established historical proposition that blacks are exceptional in American society (on this proposition, see most recently Stuckey, 1987) and the social science literature on black political culture and racial group consciousness, which suggests that the race cleavage in American society is more important than class differences and is a better predictor of attitudes and behavior among blacks (Shingles, 1981; Jackman and Jackman, 1983:48–53 ; Walton, 1985:21–42).

Apart from these studies of class differences in black opinion, there are interracial studies of opinion and attitudes in areas such as political socialization (Engstrom, 1970; Abramson, 1977), political trust and alienation (Aberbach and Walker, 1970a, Seltzer and Smith, 1986–87), ideology (Nie, Verba, and Petrocik, 1976: 253–56; Hamilton, 1982; Seltzer and Smith, 1985b), civil liberties (Herson, 1975; Corbett, 1982; Seltzer and Smith, 1985a) and attitudes toward race relations in the post civil rights era (Schuman, Steeth, and Bobo, 1985). These studies, usually employing what Farley and Allen (1986:6) call the "race-differences paradigm," are to some extent characterized by the same problems of inadequate black sample sizes and atheoretical formulation, but in addition the race-differences paradigm itself raises serious questions of comparability (especially when it is employed atheoretically), given the socioeconomic and power differentials between blacks and whites in the United States. As Gordon and Rollock (1987;15) write:

> The state of much of our comparative knowledge in the social sciences is a labile one. Furthermore, we lack ade-

quate data and understanding of the behaviors of the groups we wish to compare, given the tendency for social science knowledge to originate in studies by and of the male European-American. Therefore, we feel that it would be in the best interest of knowledge production that greater emphasis be given to intra-group studies than to between-group comparisons until these inadequacies are remedied. In particular, we need to know about sub-groups within Black, Hispanic, and Native American populations. It may well be that the differences within any one group are greater than the differences between any two. On the other hand, mechanisms or meanings of their behaviors may be so different as to make compar-isons meaningless or easily subject to distortion.

This book attempts to build on the literature of Afro-Ameri-can mass opinion since Marx's 1967 study, but also to avoid some of its limitations in terms of inadequate sample size, faulty theo-retical formulations, and atheoretical use of the race-differences paradigm. We use Milton Gordon's "ethclass" concept to analyze interracial differences in opinion. Once this is done we are in a position to identify attitudes that may be constitutive of elements of Afro-American mass culture. We then move beyond the race-differences paradigm to explore in detail subgroup opinion in black America in terms of class, region, religion, and gender.

Much ethnic difference in opinion in the United States is thought to be largely a function of class differences, often mea-sured by differences in education, but also sometimes by income or occupation differences or indices constituted by these vari-ables. Since in most modern societies ethnic or racial groups tend to be differentially distributed in the class structure, puta-tive ethnic differences in opinion or political participation are observed. This tendency of ethnic status and social class to be conjoined requires theoretical and methodological apparatus adequate to disentangle the independent effects of ethnic and class factors. Gordon's ethclass concept is a useful starting point for the purpose of this kind of analysis.

The concept is used by Gordon to characterize "the portion of social space created by the intersection of the ethnic group with social class" (1964;51). This is somewhat akin to Banfield and Wilson's "ethos" concept, which sees the tendency of per-sons to hold particular views as a function of their participation in subcultures that are definable in both ethnic and class (measured by income) terms (Banfield and Wilson, 1964, 1971). Using this concept in analyzing interracial differences in opinion in the United States yields three possible categories. First, there are the clusters of attitudes where there are no observed racial or class differences, a category we label generally "shared American culture." The second cluster of opinions is those defined in class terms, where respondents, black or white, hold opinions in common based on similar class characteristics. The final cluster of opinions is those held in common by members of a particular racial group, without respect to their class characteristics. This final set of opinions we see as racial group cultural differences. That is, differences in opinion and behavior not explained by class may represent the effects of ethnic culture, at least this is the inference we make. We discuss the rationale for this approach to mass cultural analysis later, but the problem of how to define or conceptualize culture is a nettlesome one, defying scholarly consensus for generations. For example, forty years ago Kroeber and Kluckhorn (1952) listed 164 relatively distinct definitions of culture. The time since then has hardly improved the situation. It is clearly useful, however, to distinguish between "material" (buildings, artifacts, and other concrete products) and "nonmaterial" (beliefs, attitudes, values, skills, etc.) aspects of culture. In a study of mass opinion using the sample survey, our concern is obviously with aspects of the nonmaterial culture, which we understand as the set of attitudes and behaviors that distinguish blacks from whites after taking into account the effects of class.

Culture, then, is about shared beliefs and values. We wish to understand what categories of people in terms of class and race organize themselves into what kinds of cultures in terms of their beliefs and values about such things as religion, trust in government or individuals, ideology, sexual morality, crime and its punishment, etc., or in terms of social and political behavior with respect to voting, lobbying, electoral activism, or organizational involvement. Woven together, these phenomena are constitutive of at least elements of politically relevant mass culture in the United States.

This definition (really operationalization) of mass culture is not wholly satisfactory, especially with respect to the black subculture. There is a longstanding debate among specialists in Afro-American studies about the existence, origins, meanings, and properties of black culture (for a sample of this debate, see Frazier, 1949; Herskovits, 1941; Patterson, 1972; Huggins, 1971;

Hannerz, 1969; Levine, 1978; Rainwater, 1966; Walton, 1985:21–42; Holden, 1973:16–25; Stuckey, 1987, Henry, 1990). Modern historiography (Levine, 1978; Stuckey, 1987) has established beyond doubt that it is silly to contend, as Patterson and others have, that blacks are a "people without a past, lack[ing] all claims of a distinctive cultural heritage" (Patterson, 1972:61; see also Glazer and Moynihan, 1963:25–85 for a view similar to Patterson's). However, this historical scholarship is ambiguous, to say the least, on how the analyst today might identify and measure contemporary manifestations of this cultural heritage, especially at the level of mass opinion. Cultures, after all, are not static, but rather are ever evolving and changing in response to material conditions.

Our resolution of the problem of identification and measurement of Afro-American mass culture is—as we indicated earlier—to infer that race group differences not explained by class are an effect of culture. This methodological approach to the study of intergroup cultural differences is certainly not without its problems and limitations, but we believe it is preferable to the alternative. The alternative is to identify a priori, on the basis of historical, ethnographic, or other sources, categories of attitudes and behavior that are thought to be distinctively black, and then using survey, census, or other data, test for the prevalence of these characteristics among blacks and whites. Although we could not locate a study where this approach has been used in the analysis of race group cultural differences, it has been employed frequently in studies of Southern culture (Reed, 1972, 1983, Degler, 1977). For example, Hurlbert (1989), in a recent test of the hypothesis of Southern cultural distinctiveness, selected "five conceptual dimensions" of white Southern culture—approval of force and violence, conservative political attitudes, conservative racial attitudes, conservative attitudes toward women, and conservative moral and religious orientations—based on historical and empirical studies of the region. Then, using the NORC–General Social Survey he was able to show that the South remains a distinctive region.

The problems with this approach for the study of black cultural distinctiveness are both conceptual and methodological. Conceptually, there is a greater consensus among students of Southern culture about the distinctive traits of that region than there is among students of blacks about the distinctive traits of this racial group. As we noted earlier, there is a long and vigorous argument among specialists in Afro-American studies about the historical foundations and properties of black culture. Thus, a priori selection of the appropriate conceptual dimensions of this subculture is much more problematic because, as Huggins (1971:17) writes, "Even those who support the idea of a separate culture most strongly are hard pressed to suggest its character or dimensions." Methodologically, the problem is the availability of adequate data to test for the prevalence of the dimensions, assuming that they somehow could be selected, however arbitrarily. Since most studies of mass culture have relied (as we do here) on general social surveys, the likelihood is that measures will not be available to test for many of the traits thought to be distinctive for a particular subculture. This has been a limitation in the study of certain aspects of Southern culture (see Hurlbert, 1989: 247, 251), but we believe that it would be even more problematic in the study of race group differences.

Therefore, our approach is to try to work around these conceptual and methodological difficulties by focusing on selected dimensions of American mass culture in general—religion, alienation, ideology, civic attitudes and participation—and then test for subcultural variations in terms of class and race, inferring that differences between the races not explainable by class are an effect of culture.[1] Although there is no work available using this approach with a survey in the study of the attitudinal and behavioral dimensions of black culture, Farley and Allen use it in their analysis of census data on black-white differences in family structure (household head type, extended family). Noting that there are two possible explanations—economics and culture—for the observed race group differences in family life, they write: "Since specific information on cultural orientations is not available in census data, we will settle for a strategy that attributes race variations in family patterns unaccounted for by economic factors to other factors. We are inclined to believe that this 'residual' category will likely include many cultural factors" (Farley and Allen, 1986:171). It is critical to note that this is an inference about an unexplained statistical residual that may represent the effect of culture. The validity of the inference, then, has to be accepted or rejected on the basis of historical, ethnographic, or other kinds of material on the cultural foundations of Afro-American society. This is clearly a limitation of the approach, but again, we believe its advantages conceptually and methodologically are superior to the alternative, offering a useful way to get a handle on the difficult problems involved in the identification and measurement of Afro-American culture at the mass level.

In an effort to make the book accessible to the widest possible audience, including undergraduates and interested lay readers, we have attempted to present a narrative that is not unduly burdened with jargon and impenetrable statistical tables and analysis. Often in studies involving survey research, the methodology overwhelms the substantive product. This we try to avoid without compromising the integrity of the work and its value to specialists in opinion research or Afro-American studies.

Hanes Walton, Jr. read the manuscript and provided detailed chapter-by-chapter comments and criticisms that we found ourselves incorporating again and again as we revised. His encyclopedic knowledge of the subject and his sensitivity to the limitations of behavioralism in the study of Afro-American life were extremely valuable in helping us to recognize the limits of the data and avoid distortions in its interpretation. John Howard also read the entire manuscript and provided useful suggestions, especially in terms of teasing out the implications of the findings for black politics in the post-civil rights era. The Graduate School of Arts and Sciences at Howard University provided support for the acquisition and initial analysis of the data. We also would like to thank JAI Press for permission to draw on "Sources of Urban Ethnic Politics: A Comparison of Alternative Explanations" (Smith, 1988) for use in this book. Finally, we are very much indebted to Scottie Gibson Smith (Robert Smith's wife) for typing, proofreading, and editing the manuscript through its several drafts.

Chapter One

Theoretical Perspectives[1]

Attempts to explain the content and sources of ethnic or racial group differences in attitudes, opinions, and behavior in the United States have long occupied the attention of students of American society. Although, as will become clear, there is considerable overlap, three relatively distinct lines of theory may be identified. Some theorists see ethnic or racial group differences in political attitudes and behavior as a function of differential group interests; others see the differences as rooted in or, more precisely, simply manifestations of different ethnic group heritages or cultures; a third school of thought views the differences as structural in origin, reflecting the differential location of groups in the class, authority, or, more broadly, "opportunity" structures of the society. Although there are important elements of congruence in the three theoretical approaches, we begin by laying out the essential distinguishing features of each and then move toward some kind of overarching theoretical perspective.

But before doing this, a note on our use of ethnicity and race. We recognize, with Jones (1972), McLemore (1972), Blauner (1969), and other students of black politics, that there may be semantic and substantive problems in using the terms *race* and *ethnic group* interchangeably, or in carrying over theories derived from studies of the experiences of European ethnic groups in the United States to study of persons of African origins. McLemore states the problem this way (1972:323–24):

> By a racial group, we are referring to those minorities in
> a society which are set off from the majority not only by
> cultural differences, but in a more profound sense by

skin color (high visibility) and near total inability of that group to assimilate into the larger society.... An ethnic group by definition is a group of people who differ culturally from the dominant population, but share enough characteristics in common with the main population to be accepted after a certain period of time.... A reading of history clearly points out that Black people as a legal and theoretical component of the American system of government have been left out of its political life—not mistakenly, but on purpose. Therefore, any theory or frame of reference dealing with Black politics must take into account the heretofore systematic and studied exclusion of Blacks from the American political system.

McLemore thus grounds his approach quite correctly in the unique historical experience of Afro-Americans as compared to European groups. Historically, this makes sense, yet conceptually it tends to confuse and inhibit comparative studies in ethnicity. In addition, as Holden writes (1973:209–10), there is an element of Anglo-Saxon chauvinism in this usage:

...it is superficial and inaccurate to simultaneously define "Italo-Americans" as ethnics but Anglo-Protestants as nonethnics. Each is as "ethnic" as the other. Moreover, I maintain that there is an implicit snobbery in the ordinary use of the term "ethnic," for it somehow implies that "ethnics" are merely those white people who somehow deviate from the "normal" cultural-political standards of the Anglo-Protestant population. That implicit snobbery has made it possible for social scientists (and others) to suppose that "ethnicity" was essentially abnormal, undesirable, and would in due course "disappear." Such estimates are wrong. Ethnicity is one of the fundamental bases of social organization and social division and is at least as persistent—and often more divisive politically—than social class.

Thus, we prefer to treat race as a category of ethnic group. There are many definitions of ethnicity and ethnic group in the literature (Isajiw, 1974) but Schermerhorn's usage is both theoretically comprehensive and empirically relevant for our purposes:

a collectivity within a larger society having real or putative common ancestry, memories of a shared historical past and a cultural focus on one or more symbolic elements defined as the epitome of their peoplehood. Examples of such symbolic elements are: kinship patterns, physical contiguity (as in localism or sectoralism), religious affiliation, languages or dialect forms, tribal affiliations, nationality, phenotypical features or any combination of these. A necessary accompaniment is some consciousness of kind among members of the group (1973:12).

This definition allows us in the United States context to subsume blacks in the ethnic category while taking account of their unique historical and structural location in the society. This also facilitates drawing on theories for comparative purposes drawn from any discrete ethnic group experience, without denigrating or ignoring the heritages or experiences of any group.

Interests, Class, and Culture

Prior to the 1960s, students of race and ethnicity in the United States generally did not employ interest group theory in their explanations of mass attitudes and behavior. Although as early as 1963, Glazer and Moynihan argued that, at least in New York City, the major ethnic groups were essentially giant interest groups (1963, 1970:17), most students have taken the position of Hawkins and Lorinkas (1970:18) that "Ethnic minorities rarely act as interest groups or parties." As a result, however, of the resurgence of ethnic activism in the 1960s and 1970s, *interest* as a theoretical perspective has gained increasing prominence in the literature.

The theoretical case for ethnic politics as interest politics is made by, among others, Bell (1975), Parsons (1975), Patterson (1977), and Cohen (1974). Bell argues that in modern society cultural differences between ethnic groups have withered away to become nothing more than "empty symbols," with little vitality or relevance to the group's political attitudes and behavior. However, these symbolic cultural patterns, while devoid of substantive content, can serve as a basis for political mobilization. This is so because, although ethnic groups in the United States may share the same culture or value system, they are differentially distributed in the social structure and as a result have or perceive themselves to have different interests that give rise to different political attitudes and modes of behavior. In Bell's language, ethnicity becomes a matter of "strategic efficacy." Bell writes that ethnic politics is

> one response in many instances of hitherto disadvantaged groups to the breakup of old and historically fused social and cultural, political and economic dominance structures and represents an effort by these groups to use a cultural mode for economic and political advancement.

Ethnicity is best understood not as a primordial phenomenon in which deeply held values have to reemerge but as "a strategic choice by individuals who in other circumstances would choose other group membership as a means of gaining some power and privilege" (Bell, 1975:171). Similarly, Cohen (1974:xviii) writes, "The members of interest groups who cannot organize themselves formally will thus tend to make use, though largely unconsciously, of whatever cultural mechanisms are available in order to articulate the organization of their grouping. And it is here, in such situations that political ethnicity comes into being." While this theoretical perspective is relatively new in the United States, it is supported by a smattering of recent research (Goering, 1971; Howitt and Moniz, 1976; Schiller, 1977; Katznelson, 1981:108–89; Smith, 1988).

To sum up, the interest theorists argue that ethnic politics is not class or cultural conflict; rather, it is interest conflict that is often masked by cultural symbolism. This cultural symbolism facilitates the articulation of group interests in situations of political conflict and competition, giving rise to differential group attitude sets and behavior patterns. Such competition is often between different ethnic class groups, but it may be between ethnic groups of similar class backgrounds, as in the struggle over schools, housing, political office, and employment observed by Katznelson (1981) in New York's "City trenches."

In contrast, the cultural theorists argue that different ethnic groups exhibit different cultures—values, beliefs, attitudes, or lifestyles—and that observed differences in attitudes and behavior are not merely symbolic, but are authentic cultural differences. This perspective has been traced to the early work of M.G. Smith (Smith, 1965; Katznelson, 1972), but in recent years it has been most forcefully stated by advocates seeking to reassert and revitalize ethnic awareness among European ethnic groups in the United States, especially among southern and eastern European Catholics. Advocates of this position (Novak, 1971; Gambino, 1974; Greeley, 1974; Krickus, 1976; Weed, 1973)—and it is an advocacy position as well as an academic one—contend that an ethnic group is best understood as a "self-perceived group of people who hold in common a set of traditions not shared by others with whom they are in contact" (De Vos and Romanucci-Ross, 1975:9). Such ethnic cultural traditions are said to include fundamental attitudes regarding sex, children, and family relations, as well as political attitudes and behavior (Novak, 1971:196–233; Gambino, 1974). The cultural theorists do not ignore structural, socioeconomic or interest-group factors rather, they argue that in ethnic studies "culture must be the key unit of analysis." In this view ethnic politics is not symbolic, what you see is what you get: the expression of ethnic (cultural) distinctiveness in political attitudes and behavior.

Finally, probably the most influential theory of ethnic group differences in attitudes and behavior is the class theory. Two broad types of class based explanations of ethnic politics may be distinguished, class and "ethclass." A number of scholars argue that what appears to be an ethnic phenomenon is really a class phenomenon based on a working class culture that is similar across different ethnic groups and that produces similar patterns of political behavior (Gans, 1962; Whyte, 1943; Milbrath, 1965:139; Verba and Nie, 1972:127; Dahl, 1961:11–86). Specifically, these writers suggest that there is no independent relationship between ethnicity and political opinion and behavior; rather, ethnic politics is an artifact of the lower middle class. The class theory, then, is that ethnic politics is not a function of differential ethnic cultures, values, or interests, but rather a function of the differential distribution of ethnic groups in a society's occupational or, to use Hershberg's (1979) term, "opportunity" structure. As Dahl (1961:54) nicely put it, "Ethnic politics is class politics in disguise."

Related to the class theory but also to the argument of the cultural and interest theorists as well is Gordon's ethclass concept. Gordon apparently developed the notion to call attention to the observed fact that in the United States ethnicity is generally related to social class, such that some ethnic groups are disproportionately middle and upper class, while others are disproportionately poor and working class. Consequently, the student of ethnicity must be careful to distinguish and specify attitudes and behavior that are class-based, ethnic-based, or based in some combination of the two. This is a potentially important contribution because heretofore, students of ethnic politics have tended to view attitudes and behavior dichotomously, as either ethnic- or class-based, with the view that distinctive ethnic opinions and behavior should wither away as lower class ethnic groups achieve middle class status. Over time in the United States, then, one would only observe class based opinions as all ethnic groups come to resemble each other in terms of distribution in the class structure. In this interpretation ethnic opinion and behavior persist only as long as class differences between ethnic groups persist.

The foregoing discussion of the basis of the ethclass construct is extrapolated from Gordon (1964). He is not specific in his book about the origins, abstraction, specification, measurement, or the logical or empirical interrelations among the ethnic and class variables. Indeed, essentially all that Gordon tells us about the concept is "the portion of social space created by the intersection of the ethnic group with social class" (1964:51). This scanty definition, without elaboration, is surprising for a concept that has become so influential in theory and research on race and ethnic relations (on the use of the concept in ethnic and race studies in the United States, see Dillingham, 1981; Nelson, 1979; Smith, 1988; Gilliam and Whitby, 1989). It is unfortunate as well, because it allows students to operationalize, test, and interpret the concept in any way they wish, which has inhibited theory building and the cumulative character of research in the field. We noted earlier (see p. xiii) that Gordon's formulation is very close to the ethos concept developed at about the same time by Banfield and Wilson in their book *City Politics* (1963:38–44) and tested and interpreted in subsequent articles (1964; 1971). Neither in the book nor the articles is Gordon's work noted, although the convergence between the two is close. Banfield and Wilson claim that their ethos formulation facilitates tests of the hypothesis that "Both the tendency of the voter to take a public regarding view and the content of that view are largely functions of his participation in the subculture that is definable in ethnic and income terms" (1964:876). More specifically, they posit the existence of two cultures or ethos, the first of which is an Anglo-Saxon middle-class one that has been "acquired" by upper-status Jews (and paradoxically, by lower-status blacks) and that is "public regarding" in its attitudes and voting behavior; i.e., it seeks the public interest or the "good of the community as a whole" rather than particularistic individual or group interests. The other is a lower-class, immigrant, ethnic (Irish, Italian, Polish) ethos that is particularistic in attitudes and behavior, taking no "account of the public good" (1963:41). Thus, Banfield and Wilson posit an ethclass phenomenon where ethnicity and social class intersect to produce distinctive subcultures, insofar as their conception of the public interest is concerned.

But, as Hennessy (1970) points out in a stunning critique, the ethos construct is so marred by problems in concept formation, logical structure, testing, and interpretation that it is nearly useless for scientific purposes; indeed, because of its enormous influence in the field it has operated to inhibit rather than facilitate progress and growth in the urban politics subfield. Hennessy's critique is too subtle and complex to do justice to it here, but for our purposes in drawing parallels with ethclass the following points are important. Hennessy writes:

> It is unclear, for example, whether the difference in the two ethos is due to ethnicity, social class or some unspecified combination of the two. Moreover, it is not clear if a combination of ethnicity *and* working class status is the origin of the private-regarding ethos. If it is a combination of the two, why should upward mobility produce a change in ethos?... Finally, the "theory" does not specify the environments in which the "mapping" or socialization process takes place; that is, what is it about immigrant subcultures which makes them more "private regarding"? Were these cultural values imprinted in the "old country" or through interaction in subcultures in this country, or what? (1970:542–43).

Hennessy's queries point toward the usefulness of the ethclass construct because, properly specified, it should allow us to move toward a measure of analytic clarity. First, ethclass tells us explicitly that *some* ethnic differences in attitudes and behavior may be the effects of the joint interaction of ethnicity and class. Second, it suggests that upward mobility should result in a change in *some* attitudes and behavior as individuals are acculturated to a middle-class ethos. On Hennessy's third point two things are suggested: First, that we should look historically to ethnic group cultures for the sources of ethnic ethos or attitudes and behavior; and second, that structural considerations (the location of ethnic groups in the class structure) in combination with historically understood ethnic-based cultural socialization patterns (in home, neighborhood, church, and media) may predispose *some* middle-class ethnics to retain attitudes and behavior in common with their lower-class ethnic counterparts. With a variant on nonclass-, nonethnic-based "core American culture," this is essentially what we attempt in our use of the eth-class construct in this study.

Given this sketch of the three major theoretical perspectives, we can now turn to the specific theoretical problem of this study, which is, How does one account for observed differences in black-white attitudes and behavior? Are these race group differences a function of class position, cultural distinctiveness, or distinct racial group interests? While the alternative theories at first blush may appear to conflict, on close examination they are complementary. The interest theorists view racial differences in attitudes and behavior as a function of perceived racial group interests, a perception that may cut across class or cultural differences within a racial group. That is, blacks and whites in the United States may share a common class and culture but also hold different political attitudes and engage in different patterns of political behavior because they believe that such is strategically efficacious in advancement of race interests, and race interests are perceived as more important than class or cultural concerns.

This approach is congruent with much of the recent research on the political attitudes and behavior of middle-class blacks in the post civil rights era. Aberbach and Walker (1970:380), using data from the Detroit Area Survey, report that upper-status blacks have become part of a "black political community" that includes persons from all social classes, and their attitudes are "more strongly affected by their sense of empathy and identification with their racial community than by their feelings of achievement or even their personal expectations about the future." In a longitudinal study using national survey data, Hagner and Pierce (1984) show a steady rise in black political conceptualization in terms of "group benefit," defined as the extent to which an individual evaluates political objects in terms of their negative or positive impact on group interests. From 1960 to 1980 Hagner and Pierce show that among blacks group interest increased from 26 percent to 54 percent, while among whites the comparable figures were 42 percent in 1960 and 28 percent in 1980. The Hagner and Pierce data show also that this rise in racial group interest among blacks was not an effect or function of class (measured by education), generation, age cohort, political involvement, or partisan affiliation. More recently, in an exhaustive inquiry into the intersection of race and class in the United States, Jackman and Jackman (1983:48–49) report that middle-class whites tend to exhibit stronger class bonds, while the black middle class exhibits a "radically different pattern" of race identification and preference that is approximately twice as high as their own class identification and preference. What these findings seem to suggest is that members of groups that are historically subordinate on the basis of an aspect of their ethnicity tend to identify with the interests of the ethnic collectivity rather than with their class or cultural groupings, especially when such ethnic interests are given salience, as in the recent case of black Americans, through movements of mass mobilization (Peterson, 1979; Smith, 1981).

Class and cultural theorists of ethnic attitudes and behavior agree that culture is an important unit of analysis, but the class theorists suggest that distinctive ethnic group attitudes and behavior will wither away as persons from various ethnic collectivities move from the working to the middle class. Gordon (1964, 1975), for example, contends that historically, massive (although not complete or uniform) acculturation to Anglo-Saxon norms and patterns has taken place in the United States as a result of the transformation in the social class locations of European ethnic groups. Whether one wishes to describe the norms and patterns as Anglo-Saxon is a matter of debate, the point is, however, that it is assumed by proponents of the class approach that the process of ethnic acculturation occurs with upward mobility, such that middle-class Americans of whatever ethnic origin come to share common attitudes and behavior patterns. Thus, class theory would suggest that middle-class blacks would exhibit attitudes and behavior akin to their white counterparts, while lower-class persons, white or black, would have more in common with their class than with their ethnic communities.

The cultural perspective either questions the efficacy of the historical acculturation process (Glazer and Moynihan, 1963; Parenti, 1967; Wolfinger, 1965) and/or suggests that in the late 1960s there was a rediscovery and revitalization of ethnic cultural heritages in the United States (Novak, 1971; Krickus, 1976; Weed, 1973). As a consequence, even middle-class ethnics display attitudes and behavior patterns in common with co-ethnics rather than with their class. Thus, one would expect middle-class blacks to have more in common culturally with lower-class blacks than with middle-class whites.

This would be the case especially since blacks constitute one of the more salient ethclasses in the United States. A disproportionately large part of the group today is not middle class, and a large part of the group that is middle class is of rather recent vintage (post-civil rights era; see Landry, 1987). Thus, one would anticipate that there might be, as the interest theorists suggest, a greater degree of identification with the ideological or policy preferences of this large lower-class segment of the group. One would also expect that among the new, upwardly mobile black middle class one would find more similarities with the lower class culturally, given that acculturation to middle-class attitudes and behavior might not yet be complete.

Thus, for purposes of a study of racial group differences in mass culture in the United States one may derive useful propositions from each of the alternative theories. From the interest approach one may propose the hypothesis that middle-class blacks will adopt policy preferences congruent with their racial rather than class group; from the class perspective we may propose that on nonideological or policy concerns middle-class blacks may exhibit attitudes and behavior similar to their white counterparts; the cultural perspective suggests that because of residual cultural attributes and/or the 1960s movement of black cultural identification and revitalization, there may be some attitudinal and behavioral patterns that cut across class lines in the black community. Finally, the ethclass variant alerts us to the possibility that given the intersection of race and class in the United States today and the relatively smaller size of the black middle class (and its recent emergence in many cases) that one should anticipate cultural as well as interest compatibility among class groupings in the black community. Thus, each of the three theories tends to converge toward a structural explanation: ethnic groups in modern society differ in attitudes and behavior, to the extent that they do, because of their differential location in the social structure, historically, at present, or both, which in turn gives rise to different interests and/or cultures. It is on the basis of this theoretical eclecticism that we proceed.[2]

The Structural Basis of Racial Differences in Mass Opinion in the United States

Ira Katznelson (1972:137) has forcefully argued that in ethnic research and analysis one should not put "the behavioral cart before the structural horse." That is, without an a priori analysis of structure it is difficult, if not impossible, to accurately analyze ethnic cultural patterns, socialization, voting behavior, or protest activity (Katznelson, 1972:145). And Van der Berghe (1967) writes, "Insofar as systems of ethnic relations are largely determined by structural asymmetries in wealth, prestige and power between groups, an inventory of cultural differences gives one a very incomplete picture of group relations. Cultural differences are frequently symptoms rather than determinants of intergroup behavior, even in systems where the distinguishing criteria of group membership are cultural" (1967:141). Important contributions to this emphasis on structure in ethnic studies in the United States have been made by Hershberg et al. (1979), Yancey, Erickson, and Julani (1976), Thernstrom (1973), and Esslinger (1974); thus it is that before turning to the survey data on the attitudes and behavior of the respondents we seek to establish a structural context for the analysis. By attempting to locate blacks and whites in the social structure of the nation, we are in a better position to interpret the data on racial group cultural patterns, interests, and political behavior.

Although he breaks slightly with this position in *City Trenches* and other recent work (1981:25–44), Katznelson suggests that structural analysis in ethnic research can best be promoted by "adhering strictly to Weber's multidimensional approach to stratification that distinguishes between the power resources of class, status and political position" (1972;154).

Although there tends to be a close correspondence empirically between class, status, and power, they are not, as Weber points out, identical; therefore, it is necessary to isolate each analytically in order to identify potential differential bases of ethnic group stratification. This is especially necessary in ethnic research since, in its extreme, Weber argues, the status dimension of power is "ethnic" (Weber, 1946:189).

Our approach in this section, then, is to analyze census and other data in order to determine the relative standing of blacks and whites in the social structure of the United States with respect to class, status, and political office.

Class

Weber (1946:181) understands a class to constitute a number of people who have in common "specific causal components of their life chances" insofar as the components affect access to goods and opportunities for income in a marketplace. Although Weber indicates that property or lack of property is the basic component of class analysis, in bourgeois society most persons are propertyless, and therefore their life chances or class situations are determined by their labor. As a result, property fails to differentiate between the masses of citizens with respect to class; rather, such persons' life chances in the market are determined by their occupations and resultant opportunities for income. Thus, in trying to locate blacks and whites in the nation's class structure the focus is primarily on occupational and income distributions. Income and occupation in modern society, however, are substantially determined by education; therefore, the educational attainments of the groups are also analyzed. In addition to these standard sociological indices of class situation, two other measures—home ownership and welfare dependency—are employed. To complete our description of the class basis of race formations in the United States, we also examine racial differences in wealth and asset ownership.

Analysis of the data in Table 1.1 shows that on the standard sociological measures of class—education, employment, and income, and with respect to home ownership and welfare dependency—the class structure of the United States is easily differentiated on race lines, with whites possessing a decidedly advantaged class position. Whites are better educated (twice as likely to have been graduated from college), and are twice as likely to be employed; when employed, blacks are much more likely to be employed in low-wage service and laborer occupations. For example, in 1980 blacks, although only about 10 percent of the civilian labor force, constituted 14 percent of operators, fabricators, and laborers and 18 percent of service workers. Differential representation was even more evident at the level of detailed occupational categories. Blacks accounted for 54 percent of all private household cleaners and servants, one-third of maids and garbage collectors, and one-fourth of nursing aides, orderlies, and attendants, but less than 3 percent of lawyers, doctors, and other highly paid professionals (U.S. Bureau of the Census, 1983:11). This higher rate of unemployment and disproportionate representation in low-wage occupations results in a substantial gap in black-white income (blacks earn 60 percent of white income) and the representation of blacks among the poor and welfare-dependent at a rate three times greater than whites.

Net worth, more than income, constitutes the real basis of class location in capitalist societies. Current census data show total net worth of U.S. households at $6.8 trillion. Blacks account for $192 billion of this amount, less than 2.8 percent compared to their 12 percent of the population. On a per-household basis, the average net worth of blacks is $3,400, compared to $39,000 for whites. This means that whites possess 12 times-

Table 1.1 Selected Characteristics on the Social and Economic Status of the Black and White Populations in the United States, 1982

VARIABLE	BLACKS	WHITES[1]
Education		
Median years	11.3	12.7
% High School Graduates[2]	79	87
% College Graduates[3]	13	25
Employment		
Unemployment	18.9	8.6
Managerial and Professional Specialty	6.1	95.9
Technical, Sales, Administrative	8.3	91.7
Support Services	13	87
Operators, Fabricators, Laborers	19.1	80.9
Income		
Median Family	$19,620	$25,470
% Families Below Poverty	34	10
% Families Receiving AFDC	38	11
% Families in Owner-occupied Homes	44	64

Source: U.S. Bureau of the Census, America's Black Population, 1982: A Statistical View (Washington, D.C., Government Printing Office, 1983).

1. The employment data for whites includes other races (excluding blacks), i.e. Asians and Hispanics. Whites constitute approximately 92% of the category.
2. Percentages are for persons 25 and older.
3. Percentages are for persons 25 and older.

the net worth of blacks (U.S. Bureau of the Census, 1984). Looking at the extremes in household wealth, 54 percent of blacks report net worth of less than $5,000, compared to 22 percent of whites. But at the top of the economic order, only 3.9 percent of black households, compared to 23 percent of whites, report net worth of more than $100,000. Black assets or wealth is concentrated in home equity (65 percent) and automobiles (11 percent), while white wealth is more diversified. In Table 1.2 data are displayed on selected household assets by race. The most basic conclusion to be drawn from the data is the relative absence of black wealth in other than the durable assets of homes and cars. In municipal and corporate bonds, money market funds, government securities, stocks, mutual funds, and certificates of deposit, black wealth is minuscule.

In summary, the data on class clearly document the ethclass phenomenon: Race and class intersect sharply to yield racial communities that are disproportionately poor and working class and disproportionately middle and upper class.

Table 1.2   Household Wealth and Asset Ownership by Race

ASSET	BLACK	WHITE
Own Home	44.0%	67%
Automobiles	65	89
Other Real Estate	3	11
Rental Property	7	10
Mortgages	.1	3
Own Business/Profession	4	14
Money Market Accounts	3	18
Certificates of Deposit	4	21
U.S. Government Securities	.1	2
Stocks and Mutual Funds	5	22
Municipal/Corporate Bonds	.3	3

Source: Adapted from U.S. Bureau of the Census, Current Population Report. *Household Wealth and Asset Ownership* (Washington, D.C., Government Printing Office, 1984): Tables 1–2.

Status

Of the three dimensions of Weber's approach to stratification, status is the most difficult to gauge empirically because it tends to be subjective and symbolic, based, as Weber (1946:187) writes, on "positive or negative social estimations of honor." And although persons may possess status on the basis of individual achievement of honor or deference, generally status is ascribed, a group phenomenon, so that in Weber's schema we refer to status-groups. Consequently, an individual's status is linked not to attainment of personal deference or honor but to the deference or honor accorded her or his group by the society. In order, therefore, to determine status it is useful to look, at least initially, at the history and customs of the society with respect to the honor or deference accorded individuals on the basis of their membership in discrete racial, religious, or nationality groups.

This approach to the problem renders our task relatively easy given the well documented history of racial and religious intolerance in the United States (Higham, 1955; Meyers, 1943; Frederickson, 1971; Jordan, 1968). This history demonstrates that the largely English founders of the republic established an ethnic-status hierarchy based on religion, nationality, and race. At the top of the hierarchy were white Anglo-Saxon Protestants (WASPs), followed by Catholics, Jews, and blacks. This ethnic status system, as Baltzell demonstrated in *The Protestant Estab-*

lishment (1964), endured into the postwar World War II period, and while there is evidence of a decline of ethnic intolerance in recent decades, this historical status system probably still forms the basis and point of departure of ethnic status differentiation in modern American society.

In 1978 the National Conference of Christians and Jews (NCCJ) commissioned Louis Harris Associates to conduct a survey of a nationwide sample in order to "provide an inventory of where America stands in its attitudes toward racial and religious minorities" (NCCJ, 1978:i). The survey provides measures of what the white Protestant majority thinks about each of the ethnic groups (Catholics, Jews, Hispanics, and blacks) and data on the attitudes of minorities toward each other. In general, the survey results show continued intolerance toward minorities by the "majority"; however, the study shows that "Catholics are widely viewed by non-Catholics in America as part of the mainstream of life in this country [and] by and large not discriminated against" (NCCJ, 1978:xv). Jews and especially blacks, on the other hand, still experience considerable prejudice and intolerance, while Hispanics have "suffered from being ignored by the dominant white community" (NCCJ, 1978:iv–xx). Thus, the results of this recent empirical inquiry tend to suggest confirmation of the historical status hierarchy in the United States, except that non-Hispanic Catholics appear to have experienced more status mobility in recent years than have Jews and blacks. (For more recent data on white attitudes toward blacks that confirm the Harris findings see Schuman, Steeth and Bobo, 1985).

Perhaps the most we can say about the status system of the United States in the 1980s was that it is ethnically stratified, with whites in a higher position vis a vis nonwhites. Thus, there is correspondence between the nation's class and status system, insofar as race is concerned.

Power

Power is measured by the extent of holding authoritative positions in society—in the United States, elected and appointed officials of government. Darhrendorf (1959) has argued that in modern society authority relations may be more important than class relations in determining an individual's life chances. We may not agree with Darhrendorf's argument in order to accept the notion that possession of authority (state power) is an important criterion of a group's location in the social structure.

There are about a half-million elected officials in the United States and an uncounted number of appointed officials who exercise the authority of the state. Systematic data are not available on the representation of blacks in appointed office nationally, however, the data reported in Table 1.3 on representation of blacks in elected office show that despite the highly publicized increase in black elected officials since the end of the civil rights era (from fewer than 500 in 1965 to more than 6000 in 1984), blacks are only 1.3 percent of the nation's holders of authority. The table reveals that blacks have achieved their highest level of representation in state and federal legislative office (excluding the U.S. Senate, where there is no black representation). But even at this highest level, at about 4 percent it is only a third of what one would expect if race did not structure the distribution of authority. Among the other categories of elected officials—state administrators and regional, municipal, and county authorities— one finds a level of representation of little more than 1 percent.

Table 1.3   Representation of Blacks in Popularly Elected Authority Positions in the United States

TYPE OF OFFICE	NUMBER OF BLACKS	% BLACKS OF TOTAL
All Elected Officials (490,200)	4912	1.0%
Federal Officials[a] (537)	20	3.5
State Legislators (7497)	317	4.2
Elected State Administers (564)	6	1.1
Regional Officials[b] (72,377)	25	.003
County Officials (62,922)	451	7
Municipal Officials (132,789)	2356	1.7
Education Officials (93,337)	1214	1.3

Source: Eddie Williams, "Black Political Progress in the 1970s: The Electoral Arena," in M. Preston, L. Henderson, and P. Puryear (eds.), *The New Black Politics* (New York: Longman, 1982): 73–108.

[a]Includes the President, Vice President, the Senate and the 435 voting members of the House of Representatives.
[b]Includes a wide variety of special purpose metropolitan or area-wide bodies that deliver a range of services such as transportation, conservation, or recreation.

While there are no systematic data on appointed offices, since appointed officials get their jobs from mostly white elected officials it is likely that their numbers in the aggregate are small. Representation of blacks in appointed office will vary by level of government, the size of the black population in a state or locality, systemic racism, black mobilization in a given jurisdiction, and which of the two major parties is in power; we expect, however, that at the level of policymaking cabinet, subcabinet, and agency heads aggregate black representation is low (see Eisinger, 1982). At the federal level, reasonably systematic data have been collected on black representation in presidentially appointed offices, and they show that in the post-civil rights era black representation has fluctuated from 2 percent in the Kennedy–Johnson administrations to 4 percent under Nixon and Ford, 12 percent under Carter, and about 5 percent in the Reagan administration (Smith, 1984a; Mock, 1982; U.S. Commission on Civil Rights, 1983). In the judicial branch, 1980s data show that blacks were 6 percent of federal judges and 4.5 percent of all judges (U.S. Bureau of the Census, 1983:12; Slotnick, 1984). Thus, here again one observes ethclass, pronounced racial asymmetry in authority relations.

We have shown in this analysis that in the United States today class, status, and power tend to coincide and that blacks and whites are not only cultural (perhaps) groups but also potential class and interest conflict groups as well. Thus, studies comparing black and white opinion and behavior must take account at the outset of these structural or systemic differences between the races. Although it is difficult to employ these differences in statistical models, simple demographic comparisons that do not take account of these structural considerations are likely to distort analysis and especially interpretation of the findings. As Walton writes:

> Behaviorally oriented researchers, in setting up experimental and control groups mandated by the scientific method, invariably developed black and white samples that were equal on demographic variables. Each sample has similar educational, economic, age, regional, housing, and social status levels. This pairing of demographic realities leads one to assume that the two groups are equal, politically and socially. Then, when the comparisons between the two groups are drawn and vast gaps inevitably emerge, explanations are sought only in terms of individual variables, which are inherent in the very nature of the behavioral approach. But the disparities might be due to the difference in the two groups themselves.... Similar demographics do not make groups equal—politically or socially.... In fact, the politics of race (systemic variables) are the determinants account-

ing for the differences and must be included with the individual ones (1985:12).

Given this analysis of the structural basis of racial group formations and before turning to a discussion of data, method, and analytic procedures, it might be useful at this point to compare selected class characteristics of respondents in the General Social Survey (GSS) with the characteristics derived from the census data reported in Table 1.4. The data reported in the table show essential comparability between the class characteristics of the populations and the respondents in the GSS. The intersection of class and race is clear. Whites in the sample are better educated and have higher occupational prestige and higher incomes. Indeed, although the correspondence is not exact between the census and sample data, the fit on most measures is very close, which promotes confidence in the validity of the findings.

Table 1.4   Selected Socioeconomic Characteristics of Respondents by Race, 1987 General Social Survey

CHARACTERISTIC	BLACK	WHITE
Education		
Mean Years	12.7	11.6
Less than High School	33.1%	25%
High School Graduate	29.6	34.2
Some College	21.4	17.1
College Graduate	16.	25.2
Occupational Prestige (Mean)	*34.8*	*42.2*
Lower	32.5	19.5
Mid-Lower	32.5	22.5
Mid-Upper	18.8	28.8
Upper	16.2	29.2
Income (Mean)	*$18,387*	*$29,606*
Under $10,000	36.9	17.
$10,000–19,999	19.3	27.
$20,000–34,999	21.2	28.1
$35,000 +	14.8	35.6

Data and Methods

In his critical assessment of the behavioral literature in political science as it relates to the Afro-American experience, Walton writes:

Another limitation stemming from comparison is that most studies are really studies of white political behavior with small or moderate samples of blacks included as an afterthought, as a curious exception, or to fulfill the dictates of the scientific method. This has created a vast behavioral literature, yielding complex interpretations and generalizations about political behavior, based on extremely small samples of the black population. These samples never reached the magnitude of the samples on which the theories abjut white political behavior are based. Nor did the limited size of the sample cause any of the behavioralists to qualify their findings. Knowledge of black political behavior rests on some of the most tenuous empirical evidence possible. But nowhere in the literature will one find discussion of this almost scandalous practice, which is below the standard accepted by the profession. (1985:12)

We employ in this study the National Opinion Research Center's 1987 General Social Survey in order to avoid the limitations described by Walton. The 1987 GSS is a full-probability sample of noninstitutionalized English-speaking persons 18 years of age or older living in the United States. In 1982 and 1987 the survey included special oversamples of blacks, 510 in 1982 and 544 in 1987. These special oversamples obviate the limitations of small samples in most black opinion studies and allow for more detailed intraracial analysis among blacks. (In 1982 the GSS included 1323 whites and in 1987, 1222.) In earlier exploratory work we used the 1982 GSS in a series of papers dealing with aspects of the problem of racial differences in mass opinion (Seltzer and Smith, 1984, 1985a, 1985b, 1987, 1991). We use here the 1987 survey because it is the most recent and because the items tend to overlap from year to year. (In a few instances, items from the 1982 survey are used because they are important to what we wish to do and they were not replicated in 1987.)

In a study of this sort we would prefer a longitudinal data base; however, the limitations of available surveys make this all but impossible. Thus, this study is limited by the context of the times and the behavior and opinions observed may be influenced by circumstances of the 1980s era in American society and politics. Although we will compare findings here with the results of earlier studies, the cross-sectional nature of the data is an unavoidable limitation, given the available surveys and the kinds of detailed intraracial analysis we wish to undertake.

A second limitation is the GSS itself as an instrument to study mass culture. First, the GSS is, as the name indicates, a general survey of attitudes and behavior, rather than an instrument specifically designed to study racial differences in mass culture. We would of course prefer a survey especially constructed to get at racial differences in mass culture, but resources for the development, testing, and execution of such a survey were not available. Thus, we make do with what we have.

A related limitation is that any survey, however designed, is a blunt tool to get at ethnic cultures. Cultures are complex phenomena, involving subtly formed and expressed interrelationships between values, beliefs, attitudes, and behavior. Even the skilled and experienced anthropologist several years in the field encounters problems that impede understanding and explanation of cultures (Banton, 1955:111–19; Whyte, 1943:3–69; Hannerz, 1969:201–10). The problem is even more difficult for the political scientists using the results of a general survey of hundreds of persons interviewed for a couple of hours. The best we may hope for here is a set of attitudes and reported behavior that may be rough indicators of cultural differences at the mass level. What is lost in the depth, richness, and detail of anthropological field studies is, we hope, balanced here by what is gained in theoretical power, systematic generalizability, reliability, and validity. Even in studies of culture the intuitive and idiosyncratic approach of the anthropologists might be strengthened if supplemented by the insights, however limited, of the systematic social survey (on this point, see also Wildavsky, 1987).

Conceptual Components of Mass Political Culture

In this section we explain the selection of the components or dimensions of mass culture used in the book, specify the variables employed as indicators, and explain their operationalization. The General Social Survey includes a large number of items dealing with a wide variety of attitudes and behavior on social and political life, ranging from the consequential to the trivial. We are interested in politically relevant mass opinion or culture. Political scientists have done the most work in trying to define and measure elements of politically relevant mass culture, beginning with Almond and Verba's now classic study, *The Civic Cul-*

ture (1965). This study attempted to abstract the "civic" culture from the broader nonpolitical national culture, as well as the more general or overarching political culture, in order to subject it to rigorous, empirical cross-national analysis at the mass level. Since it is often confused, it is important to point out that in Almond and Verba's formulation the civic culture is not equivalent to the political culture; rather, it is a specific component of political culture dealing with the relative presence or absence, between nations or among subgroups within a single nation, of allegiant and participant attitudes and behavior. Although Almond and Verba's work has been subjected to extensive theoretical and methodological critiques (see, for example, Lijphart, 1980; Pateman, 1980; Wiatr, 1980; and Natchez, 1985:124–50),[3] it remains the seminal work in the scientific study of mass political culture and has shaped the sparse number of studies dealing specifically with Afro-American political culture. For example, Marvick (1965) and Morris (1975:119–45), using the civic culture approach, found evidence for the existence of a distinct black political subculture on the basis of differences in black and white responses to items dealing with knowledge of politics, affective and evaluative orientations toward the political system, and modes of political participation. Thus, we believe that the civic culture is an important dimension to include in a study of contemporary mass political culture.

A second component of obvious relevance to political culture in the United States today is ideology—how citizens organize themselves along the routine liberal-conservative axis of partisan politics. As we discuss in chapter 2, the concept of ideology, as used in modern political science, is not without its share of conceptual and measurement problems; these problems notwithstanding, the broad notions of liberal and conservative are helpful in distinguishing mass and elite opinion in the United States and, the available evidence suggests, are an important feature that distinguishes black and white mass opinion. We divide this component into three discrete subdimensions involving attitudes toward government economic activities (spending and social welfare policies), defense and foreign policy, and attitudes about sociocultural or lifestyle issues. One might think that in a modern, postindustrial society cultural or lifestyle preferences in such things as sex, drug use, marriage, family, etc., would not be politically relevant.[4] But in fact, in the United States today opinion on these issues of intimacy and privacy constitutes an important cleavage, dividing Americans on the basis of age, gender, class, and ethnicity, and frequently playing an important role in partisan political choice. Barone (1990) argues that these cultural factors or personal values have become more important than economic issues in influencing how Americans vote. And it is frequently argued by students of ethnic and race relations in the United States that these socio-cultural attitudes are not only politically relevant (see Novak, 1971:196–233; Gambino, 1974; Loury, 1985; Wilson, 1987:63–92) but a key to understanding ethnic political cleavages. Thus, we include these cultural factors in the ideological dimension of mass political culture.[5]

The final two components of mass political culture that we have selected—alienation and religiosity—are less obviously politically relevant, but we think they are nevertheless important and arguably becoming increasingly so in postindustrial societies. Alienation—a sense of apartness from the social structure and a distrust of its institutions as well as of others—has long been considered of political significance because it is thought to constitute a possible attitudinal basis for political apathy, or alternatively, for movements of radical social and political activism (the classic statement of this view in American social science is Merton, 1949). Although religion or religiosity, according to both Marxist and liberal social theory, ought to have withered away as a political force in postindustrial society, it obviously has not, and in the United States in recent years it has in fact experienced a resurgence as a political factor in the life of the country. We therefore believe it constitutes a dimension of mass culture that is relevant generally in American politics, and specifically to an exploration of possible race group differences, given the often discussed centrality of religion and the church in black political culture.

The four components of mass culture we have selected here obviously do not exhaust the possibilities either in general or specifically in terms of items that might have been taken from the General Social Survey. Others with different perspectives or instruments might come up with a different configuration of components. With a phenomenon as complex as the political culture of a nation as diverse as the United States, there is probably no conceptual schema or methodological instrument that would yield a consensus on its dimensions or components. Therefore, we are satisfied that the criteria for selection of the components are clear and unambiguous; that they tap *some* important components of the phenomenon; and that they are useful in identifying areas where black-white political distinctiveness in the political culture may exist, and thus are of some relevance in explaining observed differences in political behavior between the groups.

Specification and Operationalization of the Variables

We turn now to discussion of the indicators for the four components and their operationalization. The General Social Survey includes a number of items on attitudes and behavior that might serve as indicators of the four components of mass culture. For example, 15 questions are used in measuring civil libertarian attitudinal predispositions and six to measure religiosity. It would be cumbersome to report the results for each of these questions, therefore, we constructed indices for variables with multiple questions. In order to facilitate reporting, analysis, and interpretation of the results we also standardized the indices, such that they range from 0 to 100. There are three advantages to these procedures. First, the results are easier to interpret and report. Second, it is easier to compare the distribution of two or more indices. Third, the 0-to-100 scale is useful because when we analyze questions that cannot be placed in an index, we may examine the percentage of respondents giving a specific response. This facilitates comparison with the 0-to-100 scales of the indices. We describe in detail how the religiosity and civil liberties indices were created. Index construction for other variables is then described in a more abbreviated fashion.

Religiosity

A four-stage process was used in construction of the index of religiosity. In the first stage we factor analyzed six questions that we believed measured aspects of religiosity. Four of these questions loaded highly on the factor: (1) How often the respondent prayed; (2) How close the respondent felt to God most of the time; (3) How often the respondent attended religious services; and, after respondents identified their religion, (4) How strongly they felt about it. These questions had different scales. For example, the first of these questions had a six-point scale and the second an eight-point scale. So in our second stage, we recoded each question such that a 0 represented the lowest possible religiosity and an 8 the highest possible religiosity. The recode of the six-point scale was as follows:

$$(6 = 0) \ (5 = 1.6) \ (4 = 3.2) \ (3 = 4.8) \ (2 = 6.4) \ (1 = 8.0)$$

In the third stage we added these four variables together. This new index could range from 0 to 32. Finally, we standardized by multiplying each value by 3.125 (100/32). Later, as a reliability check, we correlated this new index with an index created by the factor analysis just discussed. The correlation was 0.92. Therefore, we believe our standardized index captures the essence of the questions that gauge religiosity.[6]

Alienation

We used three different indices to measure alienation. First, we created a satisfaction index from questions that asked respondents how satisfied they were with the city or place where they lived, their nonworking activities or hobbies, friendships, their health and physical condition, their family finances, their work, and their overall happiness. Second, we employed two questions in an index to measure "general" alienation: Whether the life of the average person was getting worse or better; and whether it was fair to bring children into the world with the way things look for the future. Finally, we measured interpersonal alienation with an index created from three questions: Whether people are helpful or are mostly looking out for themselves; whether most people would try to take advantage of you if they got a chance; and whether people can be trusted.

The Civic Culture

Thirteen indices were used to measure attitudes and behavior related to the civic culture. Three questions were combined to measure political trust: How much one could trust local officials; how much one could trust federal officials; and whether public officials are really interested in the problems of the average person. Political efficacy was measured by an index created from two questions: How much influence people have over local government decisions, and how much attention one could expect from the local government in response to a complaint. The GSS includes one question asking how interested respondents were in politics and national affairs (Interest). Three questions were asked that measured respondents' knowledge of politics: Whether they knew the names of their governor, their congressman, and the head of the local school system. A series of questions was asked about membership in different organizations: fraternity groups, service clubs, veteran's groups, political clubs, labor unions, sports groups, and so on. Respondents were asked whether they were members of any groups that tried to solve individual or community problems, whether they had ever done active work (leadership, organizing, being an officer, or giving time or money) for a group, and the extent to which they had done active work in general. We created four indices in accordance with the four types of variables listed (organizational membership, membership in political organizations, activity in organizations, and leadership in organizations). Two questions about lobbying were combined into one index—Whether the respondent had ever lobbied a local government official or any other official. Two questions were asked about problem solving: Whether the respondent had ever worked with others to try to solve some community problems; and whether the respondent had ever taken part in forming a new organization or group to try to solve some community problems. Four questions asked about respondents' participation in electoral politics (beyond voting) were used to construct an index of electoral activism: Whether they had ever worked in a political campaign; whether they had attended any political meeting or rally within the last three or four years; and whether within the last three or four years they had contributed money to a political party or candidate. Finally, eligible respondents were asked whether they voted in the 1984 presidential election and how often they voted in local elections.

Ideology

Ideology in American politics as a concept and in practice is discussed in detail in subsequent chapters; here it should suffice to note that we understood the concept operationally in terms of the familiar liberalism-conservatism cleavage on the role of government, attitudes toward domestic and military spending, social welfare, social issues, civil liberties, redistributionist policies, and foreign policy. Our first measure was subjective; it involved respondents' locating themselves on a seven-point liberalism-conservatism scale (Self-Identified Ideology). Given respondents' subjective, self-identified ideological predisposition, we then located them in terms of three relatively distinct issue areas—

Economic Policy, Social Policy, and Foreign and Defense Policy. The General Social Survey asks a large number of questions about whether spending by the government is about right, too much, or too little on a series of programs or problems. Through exploratory factor analysis, two distinct factors were discerned. The first represented spending on social programs—environment, health, cities, drugs, education, blacks, welfare, and parks. The second factor concerned defense and highways and bridges. Thus, we included attitudes toward spending on domestic programs in the Economic Liberalism issue arena, defining responses that government is spending too little as liberal. Also in this issue arena we included questions on governmental policies to reduce income differences between rich and poor and whether government should do more to improve the living standards of all Americans. Responses indicating government should do more in each of these areas were interpreted as liberal.

In the Social Liberalism arena an index on attitudes toward the circumstances under which abortions should be permitted was included along with attitudes about legalization of drugs, homosexuality, pre- and extramartial sex, school prayer, and crime and its punishment. The civil liberties index was also analyzed under this issue rubric. As already mentioned, the GSS includes 15 questions that measure attitudes toward civil liberties. Respondents were asked whether the rights of five groups (atheists, racists, communists, militarists, and homosexuals) should be restricted. Three different restrictions were used: not allowing such a person to teach in a college or university; Not allowing such a person to make a speech in the community; and removing a book written by such a person from the public library. The civil liberties index was created by counting the number of times the respondent supported one of the 15 restrictive measures. Thus, respondents' scores could range from 0 to 15. In the second stage, this variable was standardized such that 0 represented solid support for civil liberties and 100 represented complete nonsupport. We then multiplied each of the respondent's scores by 6.67 (6.67 x 0 = 0; 6.67 x 15 = 100). The GSS, unfortunately, includes only a limited number of items dealing with foreign or national security issues. We included in the Foreign Policy arena an item dealing with attitudes toward communism and the defense and space spending items discussed earlier. Responses that displayed a less hostile attitude toward communism and favor less spending on the military and space were defined as liberal.[7]

Race and Class

Finally, the two major variables of concern were race and class. Race was operationalized in terms of respondents' self-classification, confirmed by interviewer verification in the context of the face-to-face interview situation.[8] Class was operationalized in several ways. Sociologists have long disagreed on the statistical and substantive measurement of social class, whether to use a single indicator, several indicators, or a sophisticated index, and, as a recent review of the controversy concludes, "We suspect that theoretical arguments concerning these issues could go on for the life of the discipline" (Campbell and Parker, 1983:452). Given this confusion in the literature, we elected to be eclectic, operationalizing class in terms of educational attainment, Temme's (1975) occupational prestige ranking, and income. Although we lean toward education as the best single indicator for class in cross-ethnic or comparative studies, given its powerful explanatory role in prior research,[9] this approach allowed us to test for the independent effects of each of the standard sociological indicators of class. We also employed a subjective measure of class—whether respondents identified their class positions as poor, working class, middle class, or upper class. Finally, we were interested in the effects of class mobility on attitudes and behavior, given its salience to the class theorists of ethnic differences. This variable was operationalized by ascertaining whether respondents' current occupational quadrant has moved or stayed the same in relationship to their father's, and if it has moved, whether in an upward direction and by how much.

In chapter 2 we begin the analysis by probing for racial differences in mass beliefs and behavior on alienation, civic culture, religiosity, and ideology, with a theoretical focus on the class and ethclass effects. Then in subsequent chapters we explore in detail the differential sources of mass belief formations in the Afro-American community.

Chapter Two

The Patterning of Racial Differences in Mass Culture

In this chapter we develop portraits in black and white of American mass opinion. This is done by isolating racial differences in attitudes and behavior. Then, in chapter 3 we examine the extent to which observed differences are the effects of class. At the conclusion of these two chapters we should have isolated four discrete opinion groupings in the United States, blacks and whites and lower and middle class. We begin with religiosity because it is postulated to have a peculiarly racial basis in history and society in the United States.

Religiosity

Faith in God, it has been argued, is perhaps the single most distinctive attribute of Afro-American culture in the United States (Holden, 1973:17). Black religious exceptionalism may possibly be rooted in the African culture and personality (Herskovits, 1941; Jahn, 1961:29–51, 96–99) but it can definitely be traced to the spirit of evangelical Protestantism and the hope for deliverance that emerged in the slave culture (Frazier, 1962:1–20; Harding, 1981; Levine, 1977:136–89; Stuckey, 1987). Contemporary studies in variants of Afro-American culture document the persistence of this religious exceptionalism. Hannerz (1969:177), for example, in his study of a lower-class black community in Washington, D.C., identified a "relative closeness to religion" as one of a number of features of ghetto life and outlook that are taken to be characteristic of this community, in contrast to what he calls "mainstream American culture." Thus, measurement of differences in religiosity is a good place to begin the search for possible cultural differences between the races.

On our index of religiosity blacks are more religious than whites, scoring an average of 62, compared to the mean white score of 52 (see Table 2.1). This ten point differential is statistically significant and suggests that on this core element of any culture, the historical relative closeness of blacks to religion persists into the late twentieth century. This is not an especially surprising finding, although there were predictions that as a result of the black nationalist and cultural revitalization movements of the 1960s and the secularizing effects of class and geographic mobility (from the rural South to urban areas), blacks might reject religion or turn to more black nationalist faiths (Islam, for example). The evidence here points to continuity and stability in black religiosity and religious affiliation.

Table 2.1 Racial Differences in Religiosity and Alienation

	BLACK	WHITE	P-VALUE
Religiosity 100 = high religiosity	62.2	52.0	.0000*
Satisfaction 100 = high disatisfaction	40.4	31.1	.0000
General Alienation 100 = high alienation	65.3	47.6	.0000
Interpersonal Alienation 100 = high alienation	72.3	43.6	.0000

*All p-values in this table based upon F-statistic from ANOVA.

Using data collected in 1964, Marx (1967; 101) reported that on most dimensions of religiosity blacks were more religious than whites. Data on denominational affiliation collected in 1957 and 1972–74 indicate that the overwhelming majority of blacks were Protestant (87 percent and 84 percent, respectively), principally Baptist and Methodist (77 percent and 60 percent), with fewer than 10 percent Catholic in either 1957 or 1972–74, fewer than 5 percent claiming no religion, and only 2 percent with a religious affiliation other than Christian (see Glenn and Gotard, 1977:444). Findings from the 1987 GSS parallel these earlier studies; the overwhelming majority of black respondents were Protestants (86 percent)—Baptists or Methodists (65 percent)—while the percentage of Catholics (7 percent), persons with no religion (5 percent) or religions other than Christian (3 percent) remained remarkably stable in this 30-year period. Thus, in the United States religious affiliation and relative closeness to religion remain an important racial group difference.[1] The sources of this religiosity and its effects on attitudes and behavior in the black community is a subject we will return to.

Alienation

It would be surprising indeed if blacks in the United States were not more alienated than whites, given their disproportionate location on the lower rungs of the modern industrial order and their status as an oppressed racial minority. Alienation, as Karl Marx and others have argued, is largely a function or effect of the dehumanization and atomization of humanity inherent in the development of industrial society (Fromm, 1967; Ollman, 1970; Meszaros, 1970). But, as Fanon (1967) has so eloquently told us, in an industrial society characterized by institutionalized racism the problem is compounded. The sources of alienation in such a society are twofold: race and class. Blacks are alienated from their labor and their being. As Fanon put it, at least the white worker, unlike his black counterpart, need not confront "the dilemma, turn white or disappear" (1967:184).

The philosophical musings of the young Marx and Fanon are supported by all the available empirical studies on race and alienation, which show, notwithstanding differences in how the concept is defined and operationalized, that blacks in the United States are more alienated than whites (Killan and Griggs, 1962; Middleton, 1963; Bullough, 1968; Olsen, 1969; Aberbach and Walker, 1969; Finifter, 1970; Wilson, 1971; Clemente and Sauer, 1976; Seltzer and Smith, 1986–87). Although the salience of race oppression as a source of black alienation in the United States has perhaps declined in recent years (Wilson, 1980), the evidence does not suggest that these changes in the racial order have substantially altered in the 1980s the relationship between race and alienation as we have come to know it (see Thomas and Hughes, 1986).

Alienation is defined and measured in a variety of ways by social scientists (Seeman, 1959; Aberbach, 1969; Finifter, 1970).

Although in the behavioral literature some attention is paid in concept formation, and, to a lesser extent, in indicator construction to the classic notions of alienation derived from Durkheim and Marx, frequently the concept is employed to mean not only isolation, disorientation, and anxiety, but also lack of trust or confidence in social institutions or other persons, as well as dissatisfaction with the quality of life at home, work, and in the community. What we try to get at in our formulation here are attitudes of estrangement, satisfaction or dissatisfaction with one's life situation, and trust in others and the political system. How does being black or white in the United States today affect one's attitudes toward the future, satisfaction with one's place in the social structure, and trust in others and in government officials? (Political trust is analyzed in the following section on the civic culture.)

In Table 2.1 data are displayed by race on our three indicators of alienation. No surprises here. Blacks on all three measures are more alienated than whites. The racial differential is especially large on the indices of general and interpersonal alienation. Black Americans are much more pessimistic about the future and much more cynical and suspicious about the motives and attitudes of others. Hannerz's (1969:177) notion that a "certain amount of suspiciousness toward other person's motives" distinguishes ghetto from mainstream culture is thus confirmed. Whether this absence of interpersonal trust among blacks is, as Hannerz suggests, a "ghetto-specific" attitude set or is more broadly distributed is an important issue for subsequent analysis. As with religiosity, it will be important to search out the sources and effects of this phenomenon on the black civic culture, ideology, and behavior, as well as to explore the interrelationship of alienation and religiosity.

The Civic Culture

Almond and Verba include in the complex of phenomena that constitute the civic culture attitudes toward the political system and attitudes toward the role of the individual in the system. Presumably, these political attitudes have some influence on political behavior. The distribution of knowledge and interest in politics, trust in government and its officials and in one's capacity to affect system outcomes may vary from society to society or group to group within a society, and measurement of such differences may provide important insights into group cultures and affect group sociopolitical preferences, as well as modes of organizational and other forms of political behavior.

In the United States blacks and whites are clearly distinguishable along these dimensions of political culture. In Table 2.2 we display the attitudinal data on knowledge, interest, efficacy, and trust. Blacks differ in a statistically significant way from whites on all four measures—they indicate less interest in politics, display less knowledge, distrust the government more and feel less politically efficacious. These results come as no surprise. What is a bit unexpected is the generally cynical, less than robust character of the American civic culture overall, even among whites, continuing a pattern first observed in the late 1960s (U.S. Senate, 1972; Lipset and Schneider, 1987). The scores from the indices do not give a full illustration of the lack of civic culture among whites. From the questions that were used to create the indices we found that among whites only 38.4 percent of respondents could correctly identify the name of their congressional representative; only 23.5 percent said they were very interested in politics; and only 39.6 percent said they trust the federal government all or most of the time. This is a bit surprising, since there had been much talk that during the Reagan presidency of the 1980s the civic culture had been renewed and revitalized, at least among majority whites. The data here, however, show that near the end of Ronald Reagan's eight-year tenure, in 1987, a

Table 2.2   Racial Differences in Civic Attitudes

	BLACK	WHITE	P-VALUE*	CONTROLS**
Knowledge of Politics 100 = high	39.4	50.1	.0000	
Political Interest 100 = low interest	46.7	38.8	.0000	
Political Efficacy 100 = low efficacy	46.9	41.2	.0000	I
Political Trust 100 = high distrust	66.9	55.3	.0000	

*All p-values in this table based upon F-statistic from ANOVA.

**Controls refer to whether or not the significant racial difference disappears after controlling for class. In this table the racial difference based upon political efficacy disappears after controlling for (I)ncome. This is discussed in chapter 3.

majority of the citizens were not interested in politics, displayed relatively little knowledge about it, and remained distrustful of political officialdom. The attitudinal differences between blacks and whites are thus more a matter of quantity than quality, which is also a continuation of the pattern observed in the late 1960s and early 1970s (Mitchell, Brown, and Raine, 1973).

In Table 2.3 data are displayed on racial differences in various modes of organizational behavior. Statistically significant racial differences are observed on all forms of activity except membership in political organizations. In terms of membership in nonpolitical organizations and organizational leadership and activism, whites are generally somewhat more participant. This finding was not necessarily to be expected, since studies of black political participation going back to Myrdal have concluded that blacks may participate more in intragroup organizational activities than whites as an alternative to interaction with whites or as a means to compensate for their exclusion from white society (Myrdal, 1944, 1967: 952–53; London and Giles, 1987; London and Giles, 1987; Guterbock and London, 1983; McPherson, 1977); as a means to escape the restrictions of or struggle against the racist social structure (Olsen, 1970; Babchuck and Thompson, 1962), or because "It requires less crossing of group bound-

Table 2.3   Racial Differences in Organizational Membership and Behavior

	BLACK	WHITE	P-VALUE*	CONTROLS**
Member Organization 100 = high	13.7	17.5	.0001	P,I
Member Political Organization 100 = high	14.2	15.7	ns	
Active in Organization 100 = high	13.5	16.4	.01	P,I,E,S
Leader in Organization 100 = high	25.3	30.9	.0007	P,I,E

*All p-values in this table based upon F-statistic from ANOVA.

**Controls refer to whether or not the significant racial difference disappears after controlling for class. For example, the racial difference based upon organizational membership disappears after controlling for either occupational (P)restige or (I)ncome. *E* refers to education and S refers to subjective class identification. This is discussed in chapter 3.

aries and because it can capitalize on group consciousness" (Verba and Nie, 1972: 171). The reader should note that organizational participation is in general quite low; less than half of the population reports membership in organizations (not including churches and trade unions), and of those, only about a third are active members or report any kind of leadership activity (these percentages are not displayed in the tables). This is a relatively low level of organizational engagement, although observers of American society as early as Tocqueville have described participation in voluntary associations as an important feature of the nation's civic culture. Here again, then, the racial differences are more a matter of quantity rather than quality in a culture that is generally not organizationally activist.

Finally, in the area of the civic culture, in Table 2.4 we show data on various modes of political behavior beyond organizational activity, including voting, lobbying, problem solving, and electoral activism. Significant differences are observed between blacks and whites on lobbying and on voting at both the local and presidential levels, but no statistically significant differences are observed on problem solving and electoral activism. The 10 percent or so gap in voting behavior is well established in the literature (Reid, 1981; Rosenstone and Wolfinger, 1981; Cavanagh, 1983) and the relative gap in lobbying (often requiring direct contact with authorities) may be explained by Verba and Nie's hypothesis regarding what they call "contacting" as a mode of political participation, in which they suggest that blacks may contact officials less than whites because it requires crossing racial lines and because of racial status group differences (Verba and Nie, 1972:164–70). We would have expected to observe also racial differences in problem solving behavior and electoral activism, given the general relationship in the United States between race and political participation. It might be suggested, but only suggested, that the absence of a significant relationship between race and these two variables is a function of racial group consciousness, as argued, for example, by Verba and Nie (1972:157–60) and Shingles (1981). But we have no way of learning this for certain.[2] In our exploration of the foundations of Afro-American mass opinion in subsequent chapters we will, however, analyze the extent to which intraracial differences in civic culture attitudes and behavior among blacks are affected by alienation, religiosity, and such demographic factors as region, residence, and gender, as well as the effect that these attitudes have on modes of political participation and ideology or policy preferences.

Table 2.4   Racial Differences in Political Behavior

	BLACK	WHITE	P-VALUE*	CONTROLS**
Lobbying 100 = high	20.0	34.5	.0000	
Problem Solving 100 = high	23.6	26.0	ns	
Electoral Activism 100 = high participation	19.6	22.0	ns	
Presidential Voting 100% = voted	64.5%	73.7%	.0002	P,I-E,I-S
Local Voting 100 = frequent voting	55.6	63.4	.0000	S,P-I

*P-values in this table based upon F-statistic from ANOVA if a scale is reported. If percentages are reported (presidential voting) the p-value is based upon chi square.

**Controls refer to whether or not the significant racial difference disappears after controlling for class. For example, the racial difference based upon local voting disappears after controlling for either (S)ubjective class or the simultaneous combination of (P)restige and (I)ncome. *E* refers to education. This is discussed in chapter 3.

Ideology

Once again in this study we are, with the concept of ideology, dealing with one of those ubiquitous yet elusive concepts that has defied common agreement on definition and measurement. As Mullins, in a fine review of the problem, writes, "Ambiguity in the concept is reflected from author to author in a wide variety of definitions, explicit and implicit, and lack of agreement regarding even the basic properties of the concept" (1972:498).[3] In the behavioral study of ideology, political scientists have employed three modes of definition and operationalization. First, respondents have been asked directly about the ideological content of their issue, candidate, or partisan preferences, as in the early work of Angus Campbell and his colleagues (1960). Second, a few students have used in-depth, extended face-to-face interviews with a small number of respondents in order to explore the foundations of citizens' world views (Lane, 1962, Bostch, 1981). And finally, in probably the most influential approach, efforts have been made to conceptualize mass beliefs in terms of "attitude constraint," the degree to which persons have a coherent structure of beliefs that reflects an underlying left-right, liberalism-conservatism dimension (Converse's 1964 study is the seminal work here).

Although there is some evidence (see Nie and Anderson, 1974; Nie, Verba, and Petrocik, 1976:110–55) of an increase in recent years in attitude constraint or issue consistency in the mass public since Converse's work (which, based on 1950s data, found hardly any), the evidence is ambiguous and muddled by differences in question items and problems of measurement. Further, even those researchers who have found an increase in ideological consistency in mass attitudes nevertheless conclude that in the United States, "Citizens are not guided in their political views by an overarching political ideology—conservatism, liberalism, socialism, or any ideology that would provide an interrelated set of answers to various issue stances" (Nie, Verba, and Petrocik, 1976:27). Instead, it seems that even in the 1980s mass beliefs were more structured on an ad hoc, issue-by-issue basis, reflecting partisanship, candidate preferences, perceptions of group interests, or the moods, biases, prejudices, and symbols that characterize what Converse (1964:241) called the "nature of the times."[4] Thus, when we refer to ideology in this work we refer not to the abstract categories discussed in classical Western political thought nor to the ideas about the role of government in society tossed around in debates by the nation's elites of politics, the media, and the academy, nor to the notion of attitude constraint. Rather, we refer to the stance on various issues that citizens displayed in responses to questions posed in the GSS. While these responses, categorized in the issue arenas of economic, social, and foreign policy, may reflect an underlying left-right ideology, outlook, or world view, we do not know nor do we mean to suggest that they do.[5] Rather, for our analytic purposes it suffices to show that respondents take the liberal or conservative positions on the issues as these are conventionally understood in contemporary partisan political debate.[6]

In Table 2.5 data on ideological self-identification and economic policy preferences are displayed. First, on self-identified ideology, blacks are more liberal than whites on both the liberalism-conservatism scale and in simple percentages. On the scale whites averaged a 51.6 conservatism score, compared to 45.5 for blacks (in simple percentages—not displayed in the table—33.5 percent of whites identified themselves as conservative, compared to 26.6 percent of blacks). These race differences, although statistically significant, are not large, especially when one considers the image in both the popular and academic literature of the black community as near-monolithically liberal in an era of increasing conservatism among the white public. For example, in their landmark study of American public opinion Nie, Verba, and Petrocik (1976:254) note that blacks had displayed liberal attitudes since systematic opinion surveys were first taken in the early 1950s. But in the 1970s, while whites were moving to the right, black opinion shifted even further to the left, leading Nie et al. to write of the "striking" character of what they described as the "extreme and homogeneous liberal opinion profile of blacks" (on the continuation in the 1980s of this ideological divergence between blacks and whites, see Luttbeg and Martinez, 1987). Two explanations may be advanced for this apparent discrepancy. First, it is probable that the word *conservatism* itself is more popular to the mass public than is *liberal,* evoking for many the notion of traditional values and ways of life. This may be seen in how these ideological labels were used in the 1988 presidential campaign. The Republicans consistently sought to pin the dreaded, unmentionable "L-word" on Governor Michael Dukakis, the Democratic nominee, arguing that Dukakis was a liberal seeking to hide his ideology from the American voter (As candidate Bush put it, "Only two things come from Massachusetts—lobsters and liberals—and he is not a lobster.") Governor Dukakis, on the other hand, until the last weeks of the campaign denied that he was a liberal, arguing that ideological labels were meaningless and that the election was about "competence," not ideology. Dukakis' avoidance of the liberal label until the final days of the campaign was apparently strategic, based on the notion advanced here that liberalism evoked negative images among large segments of the electorate.

Although Dukakis was unsuccessful in his campaign argument that the ideological labels *liberal* and *conservative* are meaningless since they are not necessarily predictive of issue positions or policy preferences, he was, insofar as the economic issue arena is concerned, largely correct. That is, the labels do not necessarily predict mass preferences on issues of economics and social welfare policy. This difference between what people say they are ideologically and what they actually believe in terms of attitudes on specific policies was first noted in opinion studies in the 1960s by Free and Cantril (1968), who observed that large numbers of Americans regard themselves as conservative but in fact are "operationally liberal" in support for specific policies and programs, especially social welfare programs. The data in Table 2.5 on support for spending on social welfare programs, government policies to redistribute income, and government programs to help the poor and the sick show the persistence of this phenomenon in the 1980s among both blacks and whites, but especially among blacks.[7] Among whites, the data in Table 2.5 show somewhat higher scores on liberalism in terms of support for social program spending than one would expect on the basis of the self identification scores (40.3 for whites compared to 51.6 for blacks), but essentially no difference on the items dealing with redistribution of income and programs to help the sick and poor, suggesting that in the 1980s ideological labels may have more issue or policy content in the economic arena for whites than in the 1960s.[8]

Table 2.5   Racial Differences in Ideological Preferences

	BLACK	WHITE	P-VALUE*	CONTROLS**
Poltical Self-Identification 100 = conservative	45.5	51.6	.0000	
Spending Social Programs 100 = spend less	20.2	40.3	.0000	
Gov. Redistribute Income 100 = conservative	31.2	48.1	.0000	
Gov. Help Poor/Sick 100 = conservative	28.9	46.2	.0000	
Homosexuality 100% = always wrong	85.4%	75.0%	.0000	
Prayer in School 100% = Supreme Court wrong	78.6%	59.6%	.0000	
Extramarital Sex 100% = always wrong	70.8%	73.9%	ns	
Premarital Sex 100% = always wrong	29.3%	29.0%	ns	
Abortion 100 = pro-abortion	49.7	59.3	.0000	I,P-E
Women Take Care Home Not Country 100% agree	33.7%	26.0%	.001	E,P

Table 2.5   *(continued)*

	BLACK	WHITE	P-VALUE*	CONTROLS**
Married Women Should Not Work 100% agree	29.0%	24.0%	.04	E,P
Fear of Crime 100% = fear to walk	47.9%	36.4%	.0000	
Courts Too Lenient 100% = conservative	77.0%	85.3%	.0000	
Marijuana 100% = not legalize	83.0%	82.5%	ns	
Death Penalty 100 = favor	48.2%	78.3%	.0000	
Civil Liberties all questions 100 = anti-civil liberties	44.5	38.9	.0001	I,E
Civil Liberties exclude racial questions 100 = anti civil liberties	43.2	38.7	.002	P,I,S-E
Communism 100 = anti-communist	72.8	81.1	.0000	
Military Spending 100 = spend less	62.1	51.2	.0000	
1984 Vote % Reagan	12.3%	65.2%	.0000	

*P-values in this table based upon F-statistic from ANOVA if a scale is reported. If percentages are reported (e.g., homosexuality), the p-value is based upon chi square.

**Controls refer to whether or not the significant racial difference disappears after controlling for class. For example, the racial difference based upon "Women should take care of the home and not the country" disappears after controlling for either (P)restige or (E)ducation. *I* refers to income and *S* refers to subjective class identification. This is discussed in chapter 3.

Among blacks, however, the labels have less meaning or issue content in the arena of economic policy. For example, blacks averaged 45.5 on the conservatism self-identification scale but only 20.2 on the social program spending scale, 31.2

on the income redistribution scale, and 28.9 on support for government programs to help the sick and the poor. This, then, is a second explanation for the discrepancy. Most studies that have found strong differences in black and white adherence to the liberal ideology have been based on specific policy attitudes on social welfare, civil rights, foreign policy, and the role and scope of government rather than on self-identification (see Nie, Verba, and Petrocik, 1976:252–56). In the economic policy arena, therefore, it is appropriate to think of black opinion as near homogeneously liberal when compared to whites.

Not so, however, when one looks at opinion on social issues or issues of personal morality, lifestyles, and values, where conservatism in terms of adherence to tradition has much more issue or policy content among blacks. Thus, when blacks label themselves as conservative, it may be, as the data in Table 2.5 suggest, in reference to this issue arena, where blacks are in fact somewhat more conservative than whites.

Looking at the distribution of responses on these issues, in Table 2.5 blacks tend to be more conservative on the acceptability of homosexuality, support for school prayer, abortion, and civil liberties (both when the question on the civil liberties of racists is excluded and included). On the approval of extramarital sex, premarital sex, and legalization of drugs the differences between blacks and whites are not statistically significant. On questions regarding the role of women in society, blacks tend to be somewhat more conservative or traditional in attitudes, with about a third disapproving of women in politics or of married women with children working outside the home, compared to about one-fourth of white respondents. Thus, black opinion here is not "extreme" or "homogeneous"; rather, the attitude sets among both blacks and whites on the range of social issues is more complex.

The issue of crime also presents a more complex set of preferences. Blacks are more likely to report fear of crime but they are also somewhat more sympathetic toward the rights of persons accused of crimes, and much more likely to oppose death as punishment for crime, by 52 percent compared to 22 percent of whites.

In Table 2.5 our two items on foreign policy show blacks tending toward the liberal side of the line, favoring less military/space spending and being a bit less hostile toward communism (72 vs. 81) than white Americans.[9]

Finally, as an ideological indicator we look in Table 2.5 at the racial distribution of the vote in the 1984 election between the conservative incumbent Ronald Reagan and his liberal Democratic challenger Walter Mondale. Clearly, white respondents are more conservative on this indicator, voting for Reagan by a margin of 65 percent compared to 12 percent black support for the President.

To summarize this discussion of ideology, blacks are more liberal than whites on economic issues, foreign policy, and voting behavior, but on social issues there is considerable variation. Blacks are more conservative or traditional on the role of women in modern society, abortion, homosexuality, and school prayer, and they tend to be less tolerant than whites of "deviant" groups in the society, such as communists, militarists, homosexuals, atheists, and racists. No differences are observed on drug legalization, extramarital sex, or premarital sex. Finally, on the issue of crime, although blacks express more concern or fear than whites they are nevertheless somewhat more sympathetic to the rights of persons accused of crimes and much more hostile to the death penalty.

Thus, black issue opinions compared to white tend to be economically liberal but socially conservative, to a degree. In subsequent chapters we will look closely at the black community in an effort to learn how these ideological predispositions are formed demographically, but we will also want to learn the effects of religiosity, alienation, and civic attitudes and behavior on defining a liberal in black America. But first, in chapter 3 we sort out the effects of class on the observed differences in black and white attitudes and behavior. Are blacks more religious, more alienated, politically cynical, civically inactive, and more ideologically liberal because of the group's disproportionate concentration in the lower class? Or is there a race or ethclass effect that bridges the class effect so that blacks of all classes share a common culture that is religious, alienated, cynical, and liberal? These are the questions we examine in the next chapter before leaving the race differences paradigm to move on to detailed study of the foundations and consequences of Afro-American mass opinion.

Chapter Three

Class and the Patterning of Racial Differences in Mass Culture

In chapter 2 we found that black Americans differ from whites on most dimensions tapped in the General Social Survey of attitudes and reported behavior. Blacks were found to be more religious, more alienated, less knowledgeable about government and politics, less interested in politics, less politically efficacious, less trusting in government, and less likely to participate in most (though not all) forms of organizational and political behavior. In general, blacks are also somewhat less likely to identify themselves as conservative than whites and are more liberal on economic and foreign policy issues. However, on social issues blacks tend more than whites toward conservative or traditional attitudes on abortion, homosexuality, the role of women, and civil liberties but are somewhat more liberal on crime and its punishment even though there is greater fear of crime among blacks than whites.

Again, there are few surprises here. Given the differential location of blacks and whites in the social structure we expected to observe attitudinal and behavioral differences. In this chapter we therefore seek to learn whether the observed black-white differences in attitudes and behavior disappear when controls for social class are introduced or whether in fact some or all of the differences remain, suggesting the existence of at least residues of an Afro-American culture or subculture in the United States. Put another way, if the large lower-class segment of the black community is statistically removed, does black opinion then resemble white opinion? Or to put it yet another way, do middle-class Americans, whatever their race, have more in common with their class counterparts than with members of their racial group? It is these questions that we analyze in this chapter.

Our procedure is to move from the simple bivariate[1] race–class relationship to more sophisticated statistical techniques that test for significant three way interactions between race, class, and an attitude or behavior. In order to get a handle on these complex interactions and to some extent simplify the discussion, we use log-linear modeling or ANOVA.[2] The basic question that we answer with these techniques is whether the addition of race (black, white) significantly ($p<.05$) improves the fit of a model that attempts to explain an attitude or behavior (e.g., liberal-conservative) by education (less than high school, high school graduate, college graduate) or any of the other class variables. In addition, these techniques allow us to determine whether or not the class effects operate differently among blacks than among whites. In order to facilitate ease of understanding, the numerical results (likelihood chi square ratios, degrees of freedom, and F values) are not displayed. Instead, the results are summarized in lay terms.

Religiosity

In Table 3.1 we display data on mean religiosity scores by race for each of our five class measures. On each of the class indicators, blacks score higher in religiosity than whites, and there are relatively few statistically significant intraracial class differences among blacks or whites.

Looking in detail at these race–class relationships, at every level of education from less than high school to college graduate, blacks are more religious than their white counterparts by a score of more than ten in each of the categories except "some college," where the spread is about half as great. There is no observed class effect either, as both higher and lower education segments of each racial group score about the same. A similar pattern is observed with occupational prestige: Blacks at all levels are more religious than whites with no observed within-group class differences. On income, except for a tendency for the highest income black group ($35,000 and above) to be less religious than others, again the same pattern of greater religiosity occurs among blacks at all income levels, with no intraclass differences among the races. On the subjective measure of class, the

Table 3.1 Class and Race Differences in Religiosity

RELIGIOSITY (100 = HIGH RELIGIOSITY)

	BLACK		WHITE	
Education				
less hs	64.4	p = ns	53.0	p = ns
hs grad	62.5		50.6	
some college	57.4		53.6	
col grad	63.0		51.9	
Occupational Prestige				
lower	64.2	p = ns	51.0	p = ns
low-mid	62.5		48.8	
mid-upper	63.4		54.2	
upper	59.2		51.9	
Income				
under $10,000	67.1	p = .001	55.1	p = ns
$10,000–$19,999	61.2		52.0	
$20,000–$34,999	62.4		51.0	
$35,000+	51.9		50.0	
Subjective Class				
lower	58.6	p = ns	45.2	p = .001
working	61.1		48.7	
middle-upper	64.5		55.1	
Class Mobility				
stayed same	63.8	p = ns	49.7	p = .06
up 1 quad	61.0		53.3	
up 2–3 quads	63.2		56.4	

Guide to Tables in Chapter 3
P-values are reported for the class differences if they are statistically significant (p < .05) or are of borderline significance (p > .10 < .05).

If an *appears next to the p-value for whites, that signifies that there is a three-way statistically significant relationship between that scale, a class variable, and race.

If a significant class effect among blacks disappears after controlling for another variable, a number is placed in superscript next to the name of the variable which is no longer significant. The number in superscript refers to which variable causes the class difference to disappear. A guide to these numbers is given below:

1. education
2. occupational prestige
3. income
4. subjective class
5. class mobility

patterning is the same except that whites who locate themselves in the middle to upper class are more religious than other white respondents. But even this group of whites is considerably less religious than its black class counterpart. Indeed, it is less religious than any black class category measured subjectively. Finally, in terms of class mobility blacks are significantly more religious than whites; among whites it is those who have experienced the greatest mobility who score highest, whereas among blacks we again see no statistically significant differences between those experiencing more or less class mobility.

In order to explore the relationships between class, race, and religiosity in a more sensitive fashion we examined the relative sizes of the inter and intraracial differences. In essence we ask, Is there a greater division among blacks based upon class or between blacks and whites (see Table 3.2)? In addition, which of the class variables exhibits the largest intraracial difference? For the religiosity index we constituted an overall score representing typical differences. The overall racial difference on religiosity is simply the difference between blacks and whites (62.2-52.0 = 10.2). The overall difference for blacks and whites on the class variables was created in a similar way. For example, for the education difference we calculated the largest difference between the four categories of the variable, usually with the result that the largest difference was between not having a high school diploma and having been graduated from college.[3] In addition, we used two other techniques to examine intraracial differences: First, the number of statistically significant relationships between each set of dependent variables and the individual class variables[4] and second, the number of statistically significant relationships remaining after controls are introduced for the other class indicators. The results are displayed in Table 3.3, indicating that the overall racial difference of 10.2 is greater than all the class variables except income (15.2), and the only significant difference remaining after controlling for the other class variables is again income. Thus, we have further confirmation of the homogeneity of black religious beliefs. The data here also suggest that income might be a better discriminator of class distinctions vis-a-vis religiosity in the black community than the other objective class indicators. The differential discriminatory power of income will be considered later in the chapter in order to determine whether high income blacks also resemble whites more than other blacks on alienation, civic culture, and ideology. If high-income blacks resemble high-income whites, this is potentially an important contribution to our understanding of the basis of class formation in black America today.

Table 3.2　Summary Differences Between Blacks and Whites
and Class Differences among Blacks (Mean Differences of the Scales)

	# Scales	Race	Educ	Occu Prest	Income	Subj Class	Class Mobil
Religiosity	1	10.2	7.0	5.0	15.2	5.9	2.8
Alienation	3	18.6	11.1	8.9	8.9	9.9	4.9
Civic Attitudes	4	9.0	17.9	16.2	10.5	5.0	9.2
Political Organization	4	3.5	23.5	19.6	9.2	5.6	12.2
Civic Participation	5	7.3	21.2	21.9	10.9	4.6	12.2
Ideological Self-Identification	1	6.1	8.6	9.8	6.3	3.4	5.6
Domestic Spending	3	18.1	4.7	5.3	6.0	5.1	3.9
Women's Rights/ Abortion	3	7.4	26.7	18.5	23.0	16.5	14.1
Sexual Freedoms	3	4.6	12.6	14.3	10.7	7.0	13.3
Fear of Crime	1	11.5	11.3	8.8	13.7	6.0	15.1
Civil Liberties/ Crime	5	12.7	11.6	7.5	13.1	4.7	6.9
Foreign Policy	2	9.6	3.5	2.4	5.8	3.6	2.6
Reagan Vote	1	52.9	9.2	4.0	9.8	2.4	6.1
Mean of 36 scales		11.0	14.9	12.9	11.1	6.2	9.0
Median of 36 scales		8.8	11.2	11.8	10.0	5.0	8.9

Analysis of these data suggests two things about the relationship between religiosity and race in the United States in the 1980s. First, observed racial group differences are not an artifact of class; blacks at whatever class level in education, occupation, and income (except for the highest) or in terms of subjective class identification and degree of class mobility are more religious than their white counterparts. Second, contrary to what the class theorists of ethnicity would suggest, religiosity was not a class phenomenon in the United States in the 1980s; rather, intensity of

Table 3.3   Summary Differences Between Blacks and Whites and Class Differences among Blacks
(Number Significant Differences Before and After Controls for Class)

	# SCALES	RACE	EDUC	OCCU PREST	INCOME	SUBJ CLASS	CLASS MOBILITY
Religiosity	1	1/1	0/0	0/0	1/1	0/0	0/0
Alienation	3	3/3	2/1	2/0	2/1	2/2	0/0
Civic Attitudes	4	4/3	3/3	3/2	3/0	0/0	1/1
Political Organization	4	3/0	4/4	4/4	4/1	0/0	5/0
Civic Participation	5	3/1	3/2	5/5	2/0	0/0	2/0
Ideological Self-Identification	1	1/1	0/0	1/1	0/0	0/0	0/0
Domestic Spending	3	3/3	0/0	0/0	0/0	1/1	0/0
Women's Rights/ Abortion	3	3/0	3/3	1/0	3/2	2/2	1/0
Sexual Freedoms	3	1/1	1/0	1/1	1/0	0/0	1/0
Fear of Crime	1	1/1	0/0	0/0	0/0	0/0	0/0
Civil Liberties/ Crime	5	4/3	2/2	1/0	2/1	0/0	1/0
Foreign Policy	2	2/2	0/0	0/0	0/0	0/0	0/0
Reagan Vote	1	1/1	0/0	0/0	0/0	0/0	0/0
Total	36	30/20	18/15	18/13	18/6	5/3	11/1

religious commitment is about equally distributed across class categories however the variable is operationalized. This means that there is little ethclass effect on religiosity. That is, the evidence here suggests that blacks are not more religious because they are disproportionately a part of a lower-class culture of religiosity in the United States today; rather, commitment to religion appears to be an element of belief that distinguishes or separates blacks culturally, to an extent. Thus, "relative closeness to religion," a phenomenon Hannerz (1969:177) identified in his field work as a "ghetto-specific trait" that separates lower-class black culture from "mainstream" middle-class culture appears to be more than that. It appears to be a *race-specific* trait that separates the black mainstream culturally from the white mainstream.[5]

Alienation

That blacks are more alienated than whites in the United States is, of course, a well-established finding of social research. However, since alienation in industrial society tends to be a function of location in the lower orders of the class structure, we would expect a good part of the observed racial difference to disappear when controls for social class are introduced. But this does not account for the entire difference, because blacks are alienated or dissatisfied not only because of their place in the class structure, but also because of their subordinate status in the racist social structure. This leads to the hypotheses that middle–upper-class whites should be the least alienated race-class segment of the United States population, lower-class blacks the most alienated, given their dual race–class victimization, and middle-class blacks and lower-class whites might resemble each other in scores on the alienation indices. Essentially, this is what we find, with some interesting twists among the Afro-American race-class groups.

In Table 3.4 data are displayed showing the scores by race-class groups on each of the indices of alienation. Among whites the results are as expected: Lower-class respondents (whether measured in terms of education, occupation, income, or subjective class identification) are more alienated than those in the middle-upper classes on each index, general alienation, interpersonal alienation, and satisfaction with the quality of life. This is especially evident in the scores on general and interpersonal alienation, where scores sometimes differ by as much as 30 points between the highest and lowest class segments. The same pattern among whites is observed in terms of class mobility. Whites who have not improved their occupational prestige vis-a-vis their parents or who advanced the least are the most alienated on all indices, but again, especially those on general and interpersonal alienation.

Among blacks the effects of class are not so clear or consistent. First, when statistically significant results are found, lower-class blacks are more alienated than middle-class blacks, whatever the measure of class or alienation employed. Second, the

Table 3.4 Class and Race Differences in Alienation

SATISFACTION (100 = HIGH DISSATISFACTION)

	BLACK		WHITE	
Education[3]				
less hs	41.9	p = .03	33.4	p = .01
hs grad	41.5		31.8	
some college	40.3		29.5	
col grad	35.6		29.2	
Occupational Prestige[3]				
lower	42.1	p = .02	35.1	p = .0000
low-mid	42.3		32.7	
mid-upper	39.5		29.5	
upper	35.4		28.5	
Income				
under $10,000	44.1	p = .0000	40.9	p = .0000
$10,000–$19,999	41.8		33.6	
$20,000–$34,999	37.1		30.5	
$35,000+	33.9		25.6	
Subjective Class				
lower	48.0	p = .0009	46.7	p = .0000*
working	40.2		34.9	
middle-upper	37.9		27.0	
Class Mobility				
stayed same	41.1	p = ns	33.1	p = .001
up 1 quad	40.7		30.4	
up 2-3 quads	39.6		27.5	

GENERAL ALIENATION (100 = HIGH ALIENATION)

	BLACK		WHITE	
Education				
less hs	65.7	p = ns	64.2	p = .0000*
hs grad	70.1		52.6	
some college	62.2		42.1	
col grad	61.6		28.3	
Occupational Prestige				
lower	66.5	p = ns	58.8	p = .0000*
low-mid	68.0		51.9	
mid-upper	65.1		49.4	
upper	63.8		33.8	
Income				
under $10,000	67.6	p = ns	61.0	p = .0000*
$10,000–$19,999	64.9		57.6	
$20,000–$34,999	65.5		45.7	
$35,000+	61.8		36.5	
Subjective Class				
lower	80.2	p = .009	67.3	p = .0000*
working	64.3		54.5	
middle-upper	64.3		40.3	

Table 3.4   *(continued)*

GENERAL ALIENATION (100 = HIGH ALIENATION)

Class Mobility				
stayed same	65.6	p = ns	50.2	p = .02
up 1 quad	64.4		48.0	
up 2-3 quads	67.1		40.1	

INTERPERSONAL ALIENATION (100 = HIGH ALIENATION)

	BLACK		WHITE	
Education				
less hs	78.7	p = .0001	52.9	p = .0000
hs grad	73.7		46.2	
some college	69.6		40.7	
col grad	60.2		33.1	
Occupational Prestige[1]				
lower	76.2	p = .002	53.6	p = .0000
low-mid	74.8		47.2	
mid-upper	70.4		41.8	
upper	60.4		34.0	
Income[1]				
under $10,000	75.4	p = .04	55.5	p = .0000
$10,000–$19,999	77.3		47.5	
$20,000–$34,999	66.5		43.2	
$35,000+	69.8		36.5	
Subjective Class				
lower	74.0	p = ns	63.2	p = .0000*
working	73.0		48.8	
middle-upper	70.3		37.8	
Class Mobility[1]				
stayed same	75.3	p = .06	48.4	p = .0005
up 1 quad	72.0		41.1	
up 2-3 quads	64.8		36.2	

lowest class segment in the black community is the most alienated of the four race–class groups. That is, as we expected, lower-class blacks are substantially more alienated than their white class counterparts. Third, on interpersonal alienation middle-class blacks (using both the three objective indicators and subjective class identification) and upwardly mobile blacks exhibit greater alienation than lower-class whites. This is also evident for satisfaction among educated and upwardly mobile blacks and for general alienation among blacks with high occupational prestige and class mobility. Fourth, on the index of general alienation there are no statistically significant class differences among blacks when the objective indicators are used,[6] although when the subjective measure of class is employed the expected pattern of greater alienation among lower-class blacks once again appears. Thus, alienation tends in the United States today to be a class phenomenon, with lower-class persons in both races being more alienated. But there is also a clear racial residue in that the most alienated race-class group is the black lower class, and on several indicators middle-class blacks resemble lower-class whites more than they do their white class counterparts. It is also interesting to note that in the black community upward mobility is only statistically significant on one of the three measures of alienation (interpersonal), whereas among whites the expected pattern is observed; the upwardly mobile are consistently less alienated. It does seem, therefore, that although alienation appears to be a class based phenomenon in the United States, there is also a significant racial residue. These results are highlighted in Tables 3.2 and 3.3. The race differences remain for all three alienation scales after class is controlled for. In addition, education, income, and subjective class have effects on one or more of the alienation scales after we have controlled for other class variables. However, race is clearly the most influential of the variables. The average racial difference for the three alienation scales is 18.6, which is substantially larger than the largest mean class difference (education, with a mean score of 11.1).

Hannerz (1969:177) has referred to interpersonal alienation, what he calls a "relative suspiciousness of the motives of others" as a trait specific to lower-class "ghetto" culture and community. The data here, however, suggest that like religiosity, alienation may be a characteristic that cuts across class lines in black America to distinguish black culture in the United States. Our analysis is consistent with the research of Thomas and Hughes (1986), in which they tested Wilson's hypothesis on the declining significance of race as a factor in black psychological well being and satisfaction with one's quality of life. Thomas and Hughes found that in the period 1972 to 1975 blacks scored consistently lower on measures of psychological well being and life satisfaction even after controlling for social class, leading them to conclude that "The significance of race as a determinant of psychological well-being and quality of life continues in spite of recent changes in the social and legal status of black Americans" (1986:830).

Two other questions deserve further consideration. First, when there are class differences among blacks, which class parallels the attitudes held by whites? Second, is the attitude structure of this class more similar to the overall attitudes held by whites or by blacks? In virtually every situation where there is a class difference among blacks and a significant difference between blacks and whites, it is the attitudes of upper-class blacks that most strongly resemble the attitudes held by whites. There were eight instances where there were significant relationships among blacks between one of the class measures and one of the alienation indices. In seven of them it was the attitudes of the highest class of blacks that resembled the attitudes held by whites,[7] although, it should be clear, not necessarily the highest class of whites. For the eighth instance it was blacks with incomes between $20,000 and $35,000 who most strongly resembled white attitudes on interpersonal alienation. For three of the eight relationships the attitudes of the higher black class is closer to the mean of whites than it is to the mean of blacks.

What these considerations show is the ethclass phenomenon. Alienation in the black community in general (with the possible exception of its interpersonal form) is in part a function of the disproportionate location of blacks in the lower class, and as this situation changes blacks come to resemble the norm of whites, although not, as the class theorists would predict, the norm for whites of comparable class characteristics.

The Civic Culture

Everything we have learned about the civic culture in the United States tells us to expect that observed racial differences in attitudes and behavior are a function of social class, and that when the appropriate controls are introduced most, if not all, the differences should disappear. This consensus on the role of social class as the most important influence on civic attitudes and participation is so strong that Verba and Nie (1972) refer to it as the "Standard SES Model." Thus, civic attitudes and behavior are largely a product of class, not ethnic cultures. Therefore, middle-class blacks and whites and lower-class blacks and whites should resemble each other in attitudes and behavior more than they resemble persons in their racially defined communities.

Yet there is an alternative to the standard SES model that posits a role for distinctive ethnic cultures that may have an effect independent of class in shaping mass attitudes and behavior. Reviewing the literature through the early 1970s on the subcultural formulation as it relates to black Americans, Morris concludes that the evidence suggests that "Race forms the basis of one of the fundamental cleavages in society which is reflected in virtually every area of political life" (1975:121). Morris then interprets the extant research to show that the black political subculture may be distinguished from the white in terms of the following attitudinal components: lower levels of knowledge and awareness; higher levels of hostility or distrust toward the government; and less positive evaluations of governmental performance. Morris argues that these cultural differences between blacks and whites in America exist because of unique race group patterns of historical experiences in the United States and because of differences between the races in the structure and patterns of socialization in the home, school, and community (1975:135–42; see also Marvick, 1965). Contrary to class theory, then, we might expect to observe differences in black and white civic cultures that are not explainable by class. Indeed, one of the principal proponents of class as a standard explanation for differences in civic attitudes and political participation—Verba and Nie—suggest for blacks a cultural component—race group consciousness—that may structure the effects of class on participation in America. Thus, at least with respect to race in the United States, both class and culture should be pursued in analysis of civic attitudes and behavior.[8]

Our findings do not support in a clear and consistent way either the class or cultural theorists of racial group differences in civic or participant culture. In Table 3.5 the data on knowledge, political interest, efficacy, and political trust are displayed by race-class groups. Among both blacks and whites political knowledge, political interest, and political efficacy are class based phenomena, with lower-class persons displaying less knowledge and interest and feeling less efficacious than the middle class. Lower-class whites (as indicated by education) score considerably higher on the knowledge index than their black counterparts (40.3 vs. 28.6), but the scores on efficacy (as well as political interest) are just about equal, with respondents of each lower-class race group scoring about 50 (using any of the class indicators) on the indicators of self-influence on the outcome of governmental decisions. Further, middle-class blacks resemble more their white class counterparts in knowledge, interest, and efficacy than they do other blacks. This class relationship holds whether class is measured by education, occupation, or income, or whether it is measured subjectively or in terms of mobility. Among blacks statistically significant differ-

Table 3.5 Class and Race Differences in Civic Attitudes
Political Knowledge (100 = high knowledge)

	BLACK		WHITE	
Education				
less hs	28.6	p = .0000	40.3	p = .0000
hs grad	40.8		51.1	
some college	43.7		52.4	
col grad	54.2		56.8	
Occupational Prestige				
lower	32.3	p = .0000	41.7	p = .0000
low-mid	39.3		47.4	
mid-upper	44.4		51.1	
upper	55.8		57.6	
Income[1]				
under $10,000	33.5	p = .001	37.5	p = .0000
$10,000–$19,999	40.7		48.5	
$20,000–$34,999	46.9		54.3	
$35,000+	47.7		55.2	
Subjective Class				
lower	35.8	p = ns	42.3	p = ns
working	38.5		49.5	
middle-upper	42.1		51.4	
Class Mobility				
stayed same	35.8	p = .0000	44.6	p = .0000
up 1 quad	45.6		53.4	
up 2–3 quads	58.0		59.8	

POLITICAL INTEREST (100 = LOW INTEREST)

	BLACK		WHITE	
Education	55.1	p = .0000	49.2	p = .0000
less hs	47.8		41.6	
hs grad	42.0		33.1	
some college	33.3		29.3	
col grad				
Occupational Prestige				
lower	53.2	p = .0000	48.5	p = .0000
low-mid	48.8		41.6	
mid-upper	42.6		35.8	
upper	31.6		31.8	
Income[3]				
under $10,000	51.2	p = .0009	44.9	p = .002
$10,000–$19,999	48.9		39.0	
$20,000–$34,999	38.8		37.2	
$35,000+	37.0		35.4	
Subjective Class				
lower	44.2	p = ns	45.7	p = .0000
working	47.8		42.5	
middle-upper	45.8		35.3	

Table 3.5 *(continued)*

POLITICAL INTEREST (100 = LOW INTEREST)

Class Mobility[1,3]

	Black		White	
stayed same	51.0	p = .05	42.5	p = .001
up 1 quad	42.0		37.4	
up 2–3 quads	42.5		33.5	

POLITICAL EFFICACY (100 = LOW EFFICACY)

Education

	Black		White	
less hs	53.7	p = .0000	50.0	p = .0000
hs grad	45.9		42.3	
some college	45.9		37.8	
col grad	36.7		34.1	

Occupational Prestige[1]

	Black		White	
lower	50.2	p = .004	48.2	p = .0000
low-mid	49.2		43.7	
mid-upper	44.9		41.1	
upper	38.0		34.7	

Income[1]

	Black		White	
under $10,000	49.0	p = .02	51.5	p = .0000
$10,000–$19,999	49.0		43.9	
$20,000–$34,999	40.8		39.2	
$35,000+	42.2		35.7	

Subjective Class

	Black		White	
lower	52.4	p = ns	58.1	p = .0000
working	46.9		43.4	
middle-upper	44.6		38.0	

Class Mobility

	Black		White	
stayed same	49.8	p = ns	44.3	p = .0005
up 1 quad	45.2		39.9	
up 2–3 quads	48.1		36.2	

POLITICAL TRUST (100 = HIGH DISTRUST)

	BLACK		WHITE	

Education

	Black		White	
less hs	67.1	p = .ns	60.6	p = .0000
hs grad	66.4		58.3	
some college	67.8		54.1	
col grad	60.5		47.1	

Occupational Prestige

	Black		White	
lower	65.3	p = .08	62.2	p = .0000*
low-mid	69.0		57.3	
mid-upper	66.7		53.5	
upper	61.4		51.6	

Income

	Black		White	
under $10,000	64.3	p = ns	61.3	p = .0001*
$10,000–$19,999	68.6		57.3	
$20,000–$34,999	66.1	53.1		
$35,000+	63.4		52.9	

Table 3.5 *(continued)*

POLITICAL TRUST (100 = HIGH DISTRUST)	BLACK		WHITE	
Subjective Class				
lower	65.9	p = ns	68.7	p = .0000*
workhng	66.8		57.2	
middle-upper	64.7		52.8	
Class Mobility				
stayed same	66.6	p = ns	57.9	p = .04
up 1 quad	66.1		53.9	
up 2–3 quads	65.8		53.7	

ences in knowledge, interest, or efficacy are not observed with subjective class identification, nor among blacks on efficacy when the upward mobility variable is employed. Otherwise, each of the class variables operates in a consistent manner, i.e., lower-class respondents have less knowledge and lower efficacy.

This is not the case, however, with political trust. Among whites lower-class respondents scored lower on trust using all four indicators of class as well as class mobility. But among blacks there were no statistically significant relationships between trust in government and social class or class mobility.[9] Blacks at all class levels display a relatively low level of trust in political authority. Indeed, with all class indicators middle-class black scores resemble more the scores of lower-class whites than their counterparts in the middle-upper classes. This finding is consistent with the results of studies conducted in the late 1960s and early 1970s, during the cutting edge of the black rebellion (see Aberbach and Walker, 1970; Mitchell, Brown, and Raine, 1973) and suggests that relatively low levels of political trust go hand-in-hand with low interpersonal trust as a characteristic specific to Afro-American culture in the United States. Overall, then, in terms of Morris' four components of a black political subculture— knowledge, efficacy, interest, and trust—only the latter appears to be a cultural effect, whereas lower levels of knowledge, interest, and efficacy appear best understood as mostly class phenomena. In Table 3.2 we see that the average racial difference for these four measures is 9.0, whereas the average differences based upon education, occupational prestige, and income are far larger. In essence, although there are substantial class differences for these three scales, the class differences do not explain all the racial differences (for three of the four scales the race differences do not disappear after controlling for class; see Table 3.3).

Turning from the attitudinal to the behavioral components of the civic culture, in Table 3.6 we first look at organizational modes of participation. The class effects are clear and consistent—the racial differences in organizational activity are an effect of the disproportionate location of blacks in the lower part of the class structure, and lower-class persons participate in organizations at a rate substantially below middle- and upper-class persons.[10] This relationship holds among both racial groups for both political and nonpolitical organizations and for levels of organizational activism, and it holds among both groups for all indicators of class (except subjective class identification) and for class mobility. Middle-class blacks in organizational behavior resemble more their white class group than their lower-class black race group counterparts.[11] A tendency is also observed in the data for middle-class blacks on some class measures to participate at a rate greater than that for comparable whites (differences are not statistically significant), a tendency first observed more than forty years ago by Myrdal.

Table 3.6   Class and Race Differences in Organizational Behavior Membership in Organizations (100 = high membership)

	BLACK		WHITE	
Education				
less hs	7.4	p = .0000	8.8	p = .0000
hs grad	12.3		15.3	
some college	15.2		19.8	
col grad	27.1		27.0	
Occupational Prestige				
lower	10.7	p = .0000	12.2	p = .0000
low-mid	12.2		13.3	
mid-upper	14.8		17.1	
upper	25.0		21.5	
Income				
under $10,000	11.3	p = .0000	11.2	p = .0000
$10,000–$19,999	11.2		14.8	
$20,000–$34,999	17.7		18.7	
$35,000+	21.4		22.0	
Subjective Class				
lower	11.0	p = .08	8.3	p = .0000
working	12.8		15.0	
middle-upper	16.0		20.3	
Class Mobility[1,2]				
stayed same	12.9	p = .001	13.8	p = .0000
up 1 quad	13.8		18.8	
up 2–3 quads	22.3		23.1	

Table 3.6 *(continued)*

MEMBERSHIP IN POLITICAL ORGANIZATIONS (100 = HIGH MEMBERSHIP)

Education				
less hs	7.1	p = .0000	7.1	p = .0000*
hs grad	11.6		13.3	
some college	15.9		19.5	
col grad	31.6		24.5	
Occupational Prestige				
lower	10.0	p = .0000	10.3	p = .0000
low-mid	11.6		12.0	
mid-upper	16.1		13.9	
upper	29.9		24.7	
Income[1,3]				
under $10,000	11.7	p = .003	10.2	p = .0000
$10,000–$19,999	12.6		13.7	
$20,000–$34,999	18.6		16.5	
$35,000+	20.8		20.0	
Subjective Class				
lower	10.8	p = ns	7.7	p = .0000
working	13.5		13.5	
middle-upper	16.5		18.0	
Class Mobility[3]				
stayed same	12.0	p = .0001	11.9	p = .0000
up 1 quad	15.5		16.9	
up 2–3 quads	25.3		22.5	

ACTIVE IN ORGANIZATIONS (100 = HIGH ACTIVITY)

	BLACK		WHITE	
Education				
less hs	6.8	p = .0000	7.1	p = .0000
hs grad	10.7		13.7	
some college	15.0		19.5	
col grad	30.4		27.0	
Occupational Prestige				
lower	8.7	p = .0000	9.5	p = .0000
low-mid	11.5		12.2	
mid-upper	15.5		14.9	
upper	27.9		26.4	
Income[1,3]				
under $10,000	11.7	p = .03	10.0	p = .0000
$10,000–$19,999	11.9		13.5	
$20,000–$34,999	17.6		16.7	
$35,000+	17.9		21.8	
Subjective Class				
lower	10.3	p = ns	6.6	p = .0000
working	13.0		13.2	
middle-upper	15.2		19.7	

Table 3.6   *(continued)*

ACTIVE IN ORGANIZATIONS (100 = HIGH ACTIVITY)				
	BLACK		WHITE	
Class Mobility[1,3]				
stayed same	11.6	p = .002	11.8	p = .0000
up 1 quad	15.3		17.3	
up 2–3 quads	22.5		24.3	

LEADERSHIP IN ORGANIZATIONS (100 = HIGH PARTICIPATION)				
	BLACK		WHITE	
Education				
less hs	17.2	p = .0000	17.0	p = .0000
hs grad	22.7		28.6	
some college	28.9		35.1	
col grad	43.3		44.4	
Occupational Prestige				
lower	19.0	p = .0000	19.1	p = .0000
low-mid	24.3		26.3	
mid-upper	28.9		31.8	
upper	44.0		43.0	
Income[1,3]				
under $10,000	23.8	p = .02	19.0	p = .0000
$10,000–$19,999	22.7		27.7	
$20,000–$34,999	30.5		33.1	
$35,000+	34.1		38.1	
Subjective Class				
lower	21.4	p = ns	15.1	p = .0000*
working	24.8		26.2	
middle-upper	28.1		36.0	
Class Mobility[3]				
stayed same	28.2	p = .0002	23.5	p = .0000
up 1 quad	26.8		35.0	
up 2–3 quads	42.0		39.9	

A similar pattern is found when one looks at other modes of civic participation displayed in Table 3.7. Lobbying, problem-solving activism, electoral activism, and voting in local elections all tend to be class-based phenomena, with lower-class persons among both racial groups less likely to engage in these forms of political behavior.[12] Except for the case of lobbying, all racial differences that occur among these variables disappear after controls for class are introduced (see Table 2.4). There is a tendency for whites at each class level of education, occupation, and income to participate more than comparable blacks, yet overall class groups resemble each other more than race groups. Behaviorally, therefore, civic participation in the United States tends to be struc-

Table 3.7 Class and Race Differences in Civic Participation

LOBBYING (100 = HIGH LOBBYING)

	BLACK		WHITE	
Education				
less hs	7.9	p = .0000	18.9	p = .0000
hs grad	20.7		30.2	
some college	21.7		43.3	
col grad	41.9		49.5	
Occupational Prestige				
lower	15.5	p = .0000	21.1	p = .0000
low-mid	16.5		27.5	
mid-upper	23.7		35.8	
upper	40.0		50.4	
Income[1,3]				
under $10,000	15.1	p = .01	23.2	p = .0000
$10,000–$19,999	21.0		30.4	
$20,000–$34,999	27.7		36.8	
$35,000+	26.4		42.1	
Subjective Class				
lower	19.8	p = ns	26.0	p = .0001
working	19.8		29.6	
middle-upper	20.9		39.3	
Class Mobility[1,3]				
stayed same	18.3	p = .03	23.9	p = .0000
up 1 quad	21.2		42.0	
up 2–3 quads	31.4		42.0	

PROBLEM SOLVING (100 = HIGH ACTIVITY)

	BLACK		WHITE	
Education				
less hs	13.8	p = .0000	15.7	p = .0000
hs grad	22.3		23.0	
some college	31.3		30.8	
col grad	34.9		36.6	
Occupational Prestige				
lower	19.6	p = .0000	18.1	p = .0000
low-mid	20.2		20.0	
mid-upper	23.7		26.9	
upper	43.8		36.9	
Income				
under $10,000	24.3	p = ns	18.5	p = .0001
$10,000–$19,999	22.5		21.4	
$20,000–$34,999	20.9		26.7	
$35,000+	30.6		31.3	
Subjective Class				
lower	17.9	p = ns	19.2	p = .01
working	22.9		23.2	
middle-upper	27.5		28.7	

Table 3.7 *(continued)*

PROBLEM SOLVING (100 = HIGH ACTIVITY)

Class Mobility

stayed same	22.7	p = .07	19.3	p = .0000
up 1 quad	26.7		30.4	
up 2–3 quads	34.3		35.1	

ELECTORAL ACTIVISM (100 = HIGH PARTICIPATION)

	BLACK		WHITE	
Education[3]				
less hs	10.7	p = .0000	13.0	p = .0000
hs grad	20.3		17.4	
some college	20.9		27.0	
col grad	35.5		33.6	
Occupational Prestige				
lower	14.6	p = .0000	14.2	p = .0000
low-mid	18.2		18.6	
mid-upper	20.7		21.9	
upper	35.0		31.2	
Income[1,3]				
under $10,000	16.5	p = .02	17.1	p = .0001
$10,000–$19,999	19.3		19.2	
$20,000–$34,999	24.8		22.4	
$35,000+	25.7		27.1	
Subjective Class				
lower	17.9	p = ns	13.5	p = .0000*
working	20.3		18.1	
middle-upper	20.6		25.8	
Class Mobility[1,3]				
stayed same	18.9	p = .03	17.1	p = .0003
up 1 quad	19.5		23.2	
up 2–3 quads	28.9		26.5	

VOTED IN 1984 PRESIDENTIAL ELECTION (100% = YES)

	BLACK		WHITE	
Education				
less hs	60.4%	p = .08	59.8%	p = .0000*
hs grad	64.2		70.3	
some college	62.0		78.8	
col grad	76.5		86.8	
Occupational Prestige				
lower	59.2	p = .006	59.1	p = .0000
low-mid	66.4		66.8	
mid-upper	62.5		76.3	
upper	82.1		87.1	

Table 3.7 *(continued)*

VOTED IN 1984 PRESIDENTIAL ELECTION (100% = YES)				
	BLACK		WHITE	
Income				
under $10,000	58.3	p = ns	62.0	p = .0000
$10,000–$19,999	64.3		69.3	
$20,000–$34,999	70.7		75.7	
$35,000+	72.3		81.2	
Subjective Class				
lower	68.9	p = ns	56.3	p = .0000*
working	66.9		68.7	
middle-upper	61.3		78.8	
Class Mobility				
stayed same	64.4	p = .08	66.9	p = .0000
up 1 quad	69.1		80.4	
up 2–3 quads	79.7		84.3	

VOTE IN LOCAL ELECTIONS (100 = FREQUENT VOTING)				
	BLACK		WHITE	
Education				
less hs	54.5	p = ns	56.4	p = .0000
hs grad	54.5		61.6	
some college	53.1		64.1	
col grad	63.1		71.7	
Occupational Prestige				
lower	51.2	p = .009	55.2	p = .0000
low-mid	56.3		58.5	
mid-upper	57.0		65.8	
upper	68.8		72.0	
Income				
under $10,000	54.1	p = ns	52.3	p = .0000
$10,000–$19,999	53.7		61.1	
$20,000–$34,999	58.9		66.6	
$35,000+	62.9		67.7	
Subjective Class				
lower	57.0	p = ns	46.1	p = .0000*
working	55.1		60.1	
middle-upper	56.0		67.4	
Class Mobility				
stayed same	54.9	p = ns	58.3	p = .0000
up 1 quad	62.0		68.1	
up 2–3 quads	65.7		72.0	

tured by class rather than race culture.[13] Consequently, in general, middle-class blacks behave more like their white counterparts than they do other blacks lower in the class structure.[14] In sum, the civic culture in the United States in the 1980s remained largely a class phenomenon, except for the important component of political trust. Black Americans are less participant than whites not as a result of some ethnic cultural residue but primarily, as the class theorists argue, because of their disproportionate location in the lower class.

Ideology

The history of Afro-American mass opinion is noted for its liberal ideology and policy preferences (Walton, 1969; Hamilton, 1982; Willingham, 1981; Smith, 1984; Jones, 1987). Yet in the post-civil rights era, with the abolition of legalized discrimination and the increased upward mobility of segments of the black community, it has been suggested that increasing ideological differentiation should be observed in the black community, with the black middle class, especially the upwardly mobile, coming to resemble its white counterpart (Ransford, 1977). This view was especially salient in the 1980s during the Reagan presidency, given the rise of a well-funded, articulate black conservative spokesgroup (Saloma, 1984:130–37; Institute for Contemporary Studies, 1981, Walton, 1988:171–74), represented by the prominent conservative economists Walter Williams (1982) and Thomas Sowell (1984) and by Reagan administration officials Clarence Pendleton of the Civil Rights Commission, Clarence Thomas of the Equal Employment Commission, and Samuel Pierce of the Housing and Urban Development Department (on Pendleton see Walton, 1988:141–43; on the views of Pierce and Thomas see Elliot, 1986:117-32, 147–66). Williams and Sowell have forcefully argued in their books, articles, lectures, and television and radio appearances that the new black middle class should rise above what they view as the parochial liberal civil rights and welfare concerns of traditional black leadership and focus its concerns on its economic class interests. Their objective class interests, they contend, would incline middle-class blacks to take the same position on issues such as the role of federal spending, private sector primacy in the economy, inflation, and unemployment as middle-class whites. As we indicated in the preface, the emergent literature on class cleavages in Afro-America and their relationship to ideology and policy preferences is ambiguous, with findings varying to some extent on the basis of how ideology is defined and operationalized, the data base used, or which indicator of class is employed (education, occupation, or income). Yet the totality of the results of the various studies seems to suggest that class cleavages in black America do not follow the anticipations of the conservative ideologues. That is, middle-class black opinion, especially on economic and domestic spending issues, does not parallel white middle-class opinion; rather, it more resembles working-class opinion, black or white, in the United States (see the papers cited in the preface by Welch and Combs, Welch and Foster, Seltzer and Smith, Tate, and Gilliam).

In Table 3.8 we display the data by race-class groups on ideology in terms of self-identification and economic issues. By using all three objective measures of class and the subjective measure we are able to address some of the limitations in the extant literature in terms of the operationalization of the class variable, and with the class mobility variable we can address for the first time in the literature the notion that it is the upwardly mobile among blacks who will be the more conservative.

The data in the table show a complex array of race-class issue-arena interactions. Although in Table 3.8 one observes a

Table 3.8 Class and Race Differences in Ideological Identification and Economic Issues

IDEOLOGICAL SELF-IDENTIFICATION - SELF ASSESSMENT (100 = CONSERVATIVE)				
	BLACK		WHITE	
Education				
less hs	48.5	p = .09	50.2	p = ns
hs grad	46.2		52.4	
some college	44.9		53.5	
col grad	39.9		50.7	
Occupational Prestige				
lower	41.5	p = .0009	50.6	p = ns
low-mid	50.3		53.2	
mid-upper	44.3		53.0	
upper	40.5		49.8	
Income				
under $10,000	45.1	p = ns	50.1	p = ns
$10,000–$19,999	44.5		52.4	
$20,000–$34,999	47.6		51.2	
$35,000+	41.3		52.6	
Subjective Class				
lower	47.7	p = ns	45.4	p = ns
working	45.9		51.7	
middle-upper	44.3		52.1	
Class Mobility				
stayed same	44.9	p = ns	52.5	p = ns
up 1 quad	46.5		54.9	
up 2–3 quads	40.9		52.9	

Table 3.8 *(continued)*

SPENDING ON SOCIAL PROGRAMS (100 = SPEND LESS)

	BLACK		WHITE	
Education				
less hs	22.6	p = ns	39.1	p = ns
hs grad	18.3		41.1	
some college	20.9		41.3	
col grad	19.1		39.4	
Occupational Prestige				
lower	22.8	p = .08	38.3	p = ns
low-mid	19.4		39.4	
mid-upper	16.7		42.1	
upper	20.6		40.5	
Income				
under $10,000	21.4	p = ns	36.0	p = .06
$10,000–$19,999	19.2		42.6	
$20,000–$34,999	17.3		41.4	
$35,000+	22.2		40.1	
Subjective Class				
lower	16.7	p = ns	33.8	p = .02
working	20.3		42.4	
middle-upper	21.3		39.0	
Class Mobility				
stayed same	21.3	p = ns	39.8	p = ns
up 1 quad	18.3		43.0	
up 2–3 quads	19.3		42.9	

GOVERNMENT REDISTRIBUTION OF INCOME (100 = CONSERVATIVE)

	BLACK		WHITE	
Education				
less hs	27.0	p = ns	41.7	p = .0000
hs grad	33.3		45.1	
some college	33.7		52.9	
col grad	32.8		55.2	
Occupational Prestige				
lower	33.0	p = ns	38.5	p = .0000*
low-mid	28.5		46.8	
mid-upper	28.5		49.2	
upper	33.8		55.2	
Income				
under $10,000	29.4	p = ns	38.7	p = .0000*
$10,000–$19,999	37.0		42.6	
$20,000–$34,999	30.8		48.3	
$35,000+	30.6		54.8	
Subjective Class7				
lower	28.6	p = .03	38.4	p = .0006*
working	34.5		45.2	
middle-upper	26.8		51.3	

Table 3.8   *(continued)*

Government Redistribution of Income (100 = conservative)

	Black		White	
Class Mobility				
stayed same	32.9	p = ns	44.6	p = .007
up 1 quad	32.5		51.8	
up 2–3 quads	29.0		51.2	

Government Help Poor Sick (100 = conservative)

	Black		White	
Education				
less hs	27.6	p = ns	40.6	p = .0000
hs grad	28.5		45.5	
some college	30.7		52.0	
col grad	30.1		48.1	
Occupational Prestige				
lower	31.4	p = ns	40.2	p = .0000*
low-mid	27.5		45.2	
mid-upper	27.0		47.9	
upper	31.0		50.4	
Income				
under $10,000	28.5	p = ns	39.7	p = .0000
$10,000–$19,999	26.8		43.0	
$20,000–$34,999	32.3		45.9	
$35,000+	31.7		50.0	
Subjective Class				
lower	26.9	p = ns	33.0	p = .001
working	29.9		46.0	
middle-upper	28.6		47.2	
Class Mobility				
stayed same	28.5	p = ns	43.6	p = .001
up 1 quad	31.3		49.9	
up 2–3 quads	26.5		50.0	

tendency for respondents lower in educational and occupational attainments to identify more as conservatives, only among blacks is there a statistically significant relationship between a class variable and self-selected ideology: Blacks of the lower-middle occupational quadrant are more conservative than others. Otherwise, neither class, measured in the several ways we employ, nor class mobility significantly affects ideological self-identification. In the 1980s, then, whether persons *think* of themselves as liberal or conservative was not a function of where they are objectively in the class structure, where they place themselves subjectively, or whether or how much mobility they have experienced. The argument of the class theorists and black conservative ideologues such as Sowell and Williams that the liberal ideology in the United States is a function of location in the lower or working class is not sustained. Rather, ideology at this subjective level cuts across class lines, with the working class being equally conservative (in terms of self-identification), if not more so, as the middle and upper classes. The great ideological divide here, then, is on race rather than class lines, and the fact that blacks identify more with liberalism than whites is not a result of their disproportionate lower-class position but rather another residue of an Afro-American political culture. The relationships are similar when one studies the data on race-class interactions on government spending. They are for both blacks and whites weak or nonexistent, suggesting that the tendency of blacks to favor more liberal spending policies on health, welfare, the cities, etc. is not a function of class. Rather, it is a racial community value that distinguishes Afro-American political culture from what some may wish to call "mainstream" majority white political culture.

There is one striking set of three-way race, class, ideological attitude interactions in the economic issue arena, and it, too, fails to sustain the hopes of the black conservative ideologues. But it does tend to support the theoretical anticipation or hypothesis of the class theorists about the lower-class basis of left-wing ideology. On the issue of whether the government should act to redistribute income, among whites it is the lower classes who are more liberal, whereas among blacks there is little relationship between the various measures of class or class mobility and this attitude. And where a relationship is observed, it is in the opposite direction from what the class theorists and Sowell and Williams would expect or wish. Unlike whites, where the middle-class groups are consistently more conservative, in the black community, where there is a significant relationship between a class indicator and this attitude, it is the self-identified working class that is less likely to support government initiatives to redistribute income. The results are similar for the item on whether the government should help the sick and the poor—lower-class whites are more liberal; among blacks there were no class-based differences.

On economic ideology in the United States, overall there is not much of a class basis. When one is observed it tends to follow the expected pattern among whites of a somewhat more liberal working class attitude set, but among blacks there are virtually no class divisions. The bad news for the conservative ideologues is not only that liberalism is a political value or residue of the Afro-American political culture cutting across class lines, but worse, when there are class cleavages, it is the working rather than the middle class that is more conservative. (We return in chapter 6 to discussion of this point in terms of the prospects for the emergence of a conservative political base in the United States.)

The complex of attitudes that we use to tap the social dimension of ideology displays a variety of race-class interactions that defy easy generalization (see Table 3.9). In the data on abortion and the role of women in society and politics—whether married women should work and whether they should be active in politics—lower-class respondents are more likely to take the conservative position; however, among blacks on the abortion attitude, two of the class variables (occupational prestige and subjective identification) did not exhibit statistically significant differences. In addition, a nonsignificant relationship was found between occupational prestige and opinion about whether married women should work. Yet in general we conclude that conservative or more traditional attitudes toward the role of women in society tend to be anchored more among the lower classes in the United States, and that black conservative attitudes on these issues are an effect of class, not race group culture.[15] (The class effects are especially strong among blacks. For example, 50 percent of those without a high school education, compared to only 8 percent of college graduates, agree that women should take care of the home and not the country.)

Table 3.9 Class and Race Differences in Social Issue Preference

ABORTION (100 = PRO-ABORTION)				
	BLACK		WHITE	
Education				
less hs	40.0	p = .0000	47.3	p = .0000
hs grad	56.3		57.0	
some college	50.8		61.7	
col grad	58.8		71.9	
Occupational Prestige				
lower	47.7	p = ns	52.5	p = .0000
low-mid	47.0		55.5	
mid-upper	53.9		59.0	
upper	55.2		69.6	
Income				
under $10,000	46.4	p = .002	49.1	p = .0000
$10,000–$19,999	50.4		56.2	
$20,000–$34,999	53.0		58.5	
$35,000+	64.7		66.9	

Table 3.9 *(continued)*

ABORTION (100 = PRO-ABORTION)

	BLACK		WHITE	
Subjective Class				
lower	51.2	p = ns	46.4	p = .0000
working	48.1		54.5	
middle-upper	52.8		64.1	
Class Mobility				
stayed same	46.7	p = ns	56.6	p = ns
up 1 quad	55.4		56.9	
up 2–3 quads	52.2		60.2	

WOMEN TAKE CARE OF HOME NOT COUNTRY (100% = AGREE)

	BLACK		WHITE	
Education				
less hs	50.0%	p = .0000	49.9%	p = .0000
hs grad	28.2		22.3	
some college	21.3		13.9	
col grad	7.7		7.2	
Occupational Prestige[1]				
lower	43.9	p = .0000	36.8	p = .0000
low-mid	34.6		32.0	
mid-upper	21.3		17.7	
upper	9.8		10.8	
Income[1]				
under $6,000	48.2	p = .0000	46.3	p = .0000
$6,000–$12,499	35.0		36.1	
$12,500–$22,499	34.8		23.2	
$22,500+	17.8		13.7	
Subjective Class				
lower	55.6	p = .0002	38.2	p = .05*
working	26.9		27.2	
middle-upper	38.9		23.9	
Class Mobility[1]				
stayed same	42.6	p = .0005	31.2	p = .0001
up 1 quad	25.0		26.1	
up 2–3 quads	16.7		12.8	

MARRIED WOMEN SHOULD NOT WORK (100% = AGREE)

	BLACK		WHITE	
Education[10]				
less hs	35.8%	p = .004	39.7%	p = .0000
hs grad	29.9		21.8	
some college	18.5		16.0	
col grad	16.9		11.6	

Table 3.9 *(continued)*

MARRIED WOMEN SHOULD NOT WORK (100% = AGREE)

	BLACK		WHITE	
Occupational Prestige				
lower	34.2	p = ns	31.2	p = .0000
low-mid	26.2		25.7	
mid-upper	22.5		22.7	
upper	21.0		12.2	
Income[10]				
under $6,000	37.8	p = .0007	38.5	p = .0000
$6,000–$12,499	40.2		33.3	
$12,500–$22,499	21.7		22.4	
$22,500+	20.0		13.5	
Subjective Class[7,10]				
lower	41.3	p = .05	25.5	p = ns
working	25.3		25.5	
middle-upper	32.1		22.4	
Class Mobility				
stayed same	32.2	p = ns	26.7	p = .06
up 1 quad	25.0		22.9	
up 2–3 quads	24.6		17.3	

HOMOSEXUALITY (100% = ALWAYS WRONG)

	BLACK		WHITE	
Education[3]				
less hs	92.0%	p = .003	89.3%	p = .0000
hs grad	86.4		84.5	
some college	79.8		68.5	
col grad	76.3		53.2	
Occupational Prestige				
lower	91.1	p = .001	84.0	p = .0000
low-mid	88.4		81.4	
mid-upper	85.4		76.2	
upper	72.4		61.9	
Income				
under $10,000	86.9	p = ns	83.3	p = .0000
$10,000–$19,999	83.5		82.0	
$20,000–$34,999	88.9		71.8	
$35,000+	79.7		67.9	
Subjective Class				
lower	86.5	p = ns	84.3	p = .0000
working	87.4		81.1	
middle-upper	82.3		69.4	
Class Mobility[12]				
stayed same	90.4	p = .02	79.2	p = ns
up 1 quad	77.1		79.9	
up 2-3 quads	83.1		71.9	

Table 3.9 *(continued)*

EXTRAMARITAL SEX (100% = ALWAYS WRONG)

	BLACK		WHITE	
Education				
less hs	75.1%	p = .07	83.4%	p = .0000
hs grad	74.4		81.6	
some college	65.7		68.6	
col grad	61.9		58.6	
Occupational Prestige				
lower	75.2	p = ns	79.1	p = .0000
low-mid	72.9		80.1	
mid-upper	62.5		76.0	
upper	64.6		62.8	
Income				
under $10,000	73.6	p = ns	78.9	p = .0007
$10,000–$19,999	68.0		77.1	
$20,000–$34,999	73.0		76.8	
$35,000+	66.2		66.2	
Subjective Class				
lower	78.4	p = ns	81.6	p = .0001
working	71.5		79.6	
middle-upper	69.0		68.8	
Class Mobility				
stayed same	74.7	p = .06	78.2	p = ns
up 1 quad	61.4		74.8	
up 2–3 quads	63.2		73.5	

PREMARITAL SEX (100% = ALWAYS WRONG)

	BLACK		WHITE	
Education				
less hs	34.0%	p = ns	43.4%	p = .0000*
hs grad	25.0		28.1	
some college	26.6		19.5	
col grad	26.9		16.6	
Occupational Prestige				
lower	31.7	p = ns	33.8	p = .002
low-mid	29.0		31.5	
mid-upper	20.3		22.3	
upper	31.7		23.4	
Income[6,9]				
under $6,000	34.8	p = .05	46.5	p = .0000
$6,000–$12,499	31.1		33.9	
$12,500–$22,499	25.0		25.2	
$22,500+	19.4		18.7	
Subjective Class				
lower	34.8	p = ns	40.0	p = ns
working	28.9		27.5	
middle-upper	28.4		28.8	

Table 3.9 *(continued)*

PREMARITAL SEX (100% = ALWAYS WRONG)

	BLACK		WHITE	
Class Mobility				
stayed same	33.7	p = ns	30.4	p = ns
up 1 quad	20.3		26.4	
up 2–3 quads	29.1		25.9	

FEAR OF CRIME (100 = FEAR TO WALK)

	BLACK		WHITE	
Education				
less hs	47.7%	p = ns	39.6%	p = ns
hs grad	45.9		35.7	
some college	45.2		40.1	
col grad	56.5		32.0	
Occupational Prestige				
lower	42.5	p = ns	37.2	p = ns
low-mid	47.8		31.9	
mid-upper	48.4		36.7	
upper	51.3		36.6	
Income				
under $10,000	55.4	p = .10	52.6	p = .0000
$10,000–$19,999	49.2		39.5	
$20,000–$34,999	41.7		38.5	
$35,000+	42.3		26.3	
Subjective Class				
lower	52.8	p = ns	43.1	p = ns
working	48.2		34.5	
middle-upper	46.8		37.3	
Class Mobility				
stayed same	41.4	p = .10	34.3	p = ns
up 1 quad	45.8		36.8	
up 2–3 quads	56.5		35.3	

COURTS NOT HARSH ENOUGH (100% = AGREE))

	BLACK		WHITE	
Education				
less hs	76.5%	p = ns	85.0%	p = .03
hs grad	81.8		88.6	
some college	72.1		86.1	
col grad	76.5		80.1	
Occupational Prestige				
lower	78.5	p = ns	87.0	p = ns
low-mid	77.9		86.2	
mid-upper	75.0		84.5	
upper	77.9		83.3	

Table 3.9 *(continued)*

COURTS NOT HARSH ENOUGH (100% = AGREE)	BLACK		WHITE	
Income				
under $10,000	75.6	p = ns	85.1	p = ns
$10,000–$19,999	75.6		87.3	
$20,000–$34,999	78.2		85.3	
$35,000+	84.3		85.8	
Subjective Class				
lower	85.4	p = ns	84.8	p = ns
working	78.4		85.3	
middle-upper	74.1		85.9	
Class Mobility				
stayed same	81.0	p = ns	85.8	p = ns
up 1 quad	74.6		86.9	
up 2–3 quads	77.3		84.3	

LEGALIZE MARIJUANA (100% = NOT LEGALIZE)	BLACK		WHITE	
Education[12]				
less hs	89.5%	p = .02	88.6%	p = .0000
hs grad	81.8		85.6	
some college	76.4		76.7	
col grad	79.8		76.2	
Occupational Prestige				
lower	80.8	p = ns	86.0	p = .01
low-mid	84.1		80.5	
mid-upper	81.6		85.3	
upper	83.3		77.3	
Income[6,12]				
under $10,000	85.5	p = .03	85.1	p = ns
$10,000–$19,999	84.9		79.9	
$20,000–$34,999	79.2		83.2	
$35,000+	70.0		82.0	
Subjective Class				
lower	86.8	p = ns	75.0	p = ns
working	81.7		84.7	
middle-upper	83.4		81.0	
Class Mobility				
stayed same	85.0	p = ns	83.1	p = ns
up 1 quad	77.6		83.3	
up 2–3 quads	82.4		82.1	

FAVOR DEATH PENALTY (100% = FAVOR)	BLACK		WHITE	
Education				
less hs	48.4%	p = ns	72.9	p = .0004
hs grad	47.9		83.0	
some college	50.9		83.8	
col grad			72.8	

Table 3.9 *(continued)*

FAVOR DEATH PENALTY (100% = FAVOR)

	BLACK		WHITE	
Occupational Prestige				
lower	47.4	p = ns	77.5	p = ns
low-mid	49.0		78.8	
mid-upper	44.9		80.9	
upper	51.3		76.6	
Income				
under $10,000	44.7	p = ns	68.0	p = .0009
$10,000–$19,999	43.1		76.1	
$20,000–$34,999	52.6		83.0	
$35,000+	58.2		80.4	
Subjective Class				
lower	46.9	p = ns	57.8	p = .0009
working	48.6		81.5	
middle-upper	48.3		77.9	
Class Mobility				
stayed same	45.6	p = ns	77.2	p = ns
up 1 quad	53.1		81.4	
up 2-3 quads	45.5		78.0	

SUPREME COURT'S DECISION ON SCHOOL PRAYER (100% = DISAPPROVE)

	BLACK		WHITE	
Education				
less hs	84.2%	p = .06	69.2%	p = .0000
hs grad	74.6		64.2	
some college	76.0		55.3	
col grad	71.0		40.3	
Occupational Prestige				
lower	79.6	p = ns	64.6	p = .0001
low-mid	80.8		60.6	
mid-upper	80.5		62.5	
upper	73.3		47.1	
Income				
under $6,000	83.1	p = ns	71.1	p = .01
$6,000–$12,499	79.2		61.1	
$12,500–$22,499	83.0		57.8	
$22,500+	72.0		56.5	
Subjective Class				
lower	77.3	p = ns	69.6	p = .02
working	79.6		62.4	
middle-upper	78.9		56.1	
Class Mobility				
stayed same	80.7	p = ns	62.9	p = .07
up 1 quad	80.7		63.8	
up 2–3 quads	83.3		53.1	

Table 3.9 *(continued)*

CIVIL LIBERTIES (ALL QUESTIONS) (100 = ANTI-CIVIL LIBERTIES)

	BLACK		WHITE	
Education				
less hs	51.1	p = .0000	54.9	p = .0000*
hs grad	47.4		44.0	
some college	40.6		33.7	
col grad	32.2		20.6	
Occupational Prestige1				
lower	50.1	p = .0002	46.6	p = .0000
low-mid	46.4		43.7	
mid-upper	43.2		41.9	
upper	33.5		25.1	
Income1				
under $10,000	48.9	p = .001	49.9	p = .0000
$10,000–$19,999	46.2		43.1	
$20,000–$34,999	43.1		38.8	
$35,000+	33.7		30.0	
Subjective Class				
lower	47.3	p = ns	49.1	p = .002
working	44.0		40.6	
middle-upper	45.9		36.7	
Class Mobility1				
stayed same	49.0	p = .03	42.8	p = .007
up 1 quad	42.2		42.2	
up 2–3 quads	39.5		34.8	

CIVIL LIBERTIES (EXCLUDING RACIST QUESTIONS) (100 = ANTI-CIVIL LIBERTIES)

	BLACK		WHITE	
Education				
less hs	50.2	p = .0000	57.1	p = .0000*
hs grad	46.3		43.0	
some college	38.6		32.3	
col grad	30.7		20.0	
Occupational Prestige1				
lower	49.3	p = .0000	47.8	p = .0000
low-mid	45.1		43.3	
mid-upper	41.5		41.3	
upper	31.9		24.4	
Income1				
under $10,000	47.9	p = .0006	51.0	p = .0000
$10,000–$19,999	44.3		42.7	
$20,000–$34,999	41.5		38.4	
$35,000+	32.4		29.2	
Subjective Class				
lower	46.4	p = ns	50.1	p = .0007
working	42.8		40.6	
middle-upper	44.4		36.2	

Table 3.9 *(continued)*

CIVIL LIBERTIES (EXCLUDING RACIST QUESTIONS) (100 = ANTI-CIVIL LIBERTIES)				
	BLACK		WHITE	
Class Mobility[1]				
stayed same	48.4	p = .01	43.1	p = .005
up 1 quad	40.9		41.8	
up 2–3 quads	37.6		34.5	

On issues of sexual intimacy—attitudes toward pre- and extramarital sex and homosexuality—with some exceptions depending on the class indicator, the tendency again is for lower-class respondents among both racial groups to be conservative, i.e., to say that such acts are always wrong. On homosexuality, no statistically significant relation is observed between income and subjective class. And although the percentages among blacks on attitudes toward extramarital sex parallel those of whites, none of the class variables is significant. This suggests that apparent racial differences (in examining statistical significance) are simply a function of disparate sample sizes.[16] Overall, then, we conclude that attitudes toward sexual permissiveness, like attitudes toward abortion and the rights of women, are class-based, and the apparent black conservatism on such matters is a function of the disproportionately large black lower and working classes and not an effect of culture.

Attitudes toward the legalization of drugs does not distinguish the races, although there is a tendency among both races for lower-class respondents to be more conservative or less permissive. Crime and its punishment, as the 1988 Bush-Dukakis presidential campaign amply illustrated, is still a most divisive social issue laden with racial overtones and undercurrents.[17] Although blacks are more likely to be both perpetrators and victims of crime and indicate a somewhat higher level of fear,[18] black opinion remains consistently more liberal on its punishment, and this liberal attitude set cuts across class lines in the community, i.e., there are no statistically significant relationships between any of the class variables and the items on crime. Among whites attitudes toward crime are more complex.[19] On the emotional death penalty issue, for example, the class variables do not operate in a consistent way. Whites with less than a high school education and whites who are college graduates are more liberal than other whites, but on the other hand, whites with higher incomes are more likely to support the death penalty than lower-income whites. Thus, a confusing picture forms for whites in terms of whether attitudes toward crime are class-based and in terms of which white class group is more liberal or conservative.

On civil liberties—attitudes toward the rights of "deviant" groups—it is well-established that tolerance is a function of education, and that well-educated persons are more likely to be supporters of civil liberties (see Nunn, Crockett, and Williams, 1978; Corbett, 1982). The data here support this conclusion. Civil libertarian attitudinal predispositions are class-based, with higher class respondents (however measured) among both races being more liberal.[20] Intolerance of groups with different views or lifestyles is a phenomenon rooted in the lower classes in the United States, and observed higher levels of black intolerance are effects of class, not culture among blacks. In fact, the racial differences that occur disappear after class controls are introduced, regardless of whether the questions on limiting the rights of racists are included.

Finally, in the social issue arena—whether one approves of the Supreme Court's 1961 decision banning school prayer[21]—among whites, attitudes are class-based. Respondents of the lower class (using all measures) are more likely to support prayer in school, whereas among blacks no class effects are observed. Blacks of all social classes disapprove almost uniformly of the ban on prayer in school. This attitude is clearly an Afro-American cultural residue, rooted perhaps in the community's religiosity (discussed earlier).

In sum, of the five questions relating to civil liberties and crime issues, there are three issues that are primarily race based (courts are too lenient, death penalty, and school prayer) and two that are primarily class based (civil liberties and drugs).

In the foreign policy arena (Table 3.10), attitudes toward military spending show weak or no class relations at all among both blacks and whites, but hostile attitudes toward communism among whites do tend to predominate among lower educational and occupational strata, whereas among blacks no class relations are observed. In this arena, then, the relatively greater degree of liberalism among blacks appears to be a communitywide attitude set and not an effect of class.[22]

As for respondents' vote in the 1984 election, there were no class differences among blacks, but among whites respondents in the upper classes (as measured by education, income, and subjective class) were more likely to vote for Reagan than for

Table 3.10 Class and Race Differences in Foreign Policy Issue Preference and the 1984 Vote

SPENDING ON MILITARY AND SPACE (100 = SPEND LESS)

	BLACK		WHITE	
Education				
less hs	61.3	p = ns	52.0	p = ns
hs grad	61.9		51.2	
some college	62.0		50.3	
col grad	63.6		51.3	
Occupational Prestige				
lower	60.1	p = ns	53.0	p = ns
low-mid	63.2		51.0	
mid-upper	62.6		50.2	
upper	62.3		50.3	
Income				
under $10,000	62.7	p = ns	56.4	p = .0002
$10,000–$19,999	61.3		50.5	
$20,000–$34,999	63.0		52.7	
$35,000+	58.5		48.0	
Subjective Class				
lower	65.0	p = ns	51.5	p = ns
working	61.5		52.5	
middle-upper	62.0		50.4	
Class Mobility				
stayed same	61.5	p = ns	51.5	p = ns
up 1 quad	61.9		49.7	
up 2–3 quads	60.8		52.1	

COMMUNISM (100 = ANTI-COMMUNIST)

	BLACK		WHITE	
Education				
less hs	71.0	p = ns	83.1	p = .0000
hs grad	75.7		85.4	
some college	71.8		81.5	
col grad	73.0		81.0	
Occupational Prestige				
lower	72.0	p = ns	84.7	p = .004
low-mid	73.3		81.8	
mid-upper	73.7		81.8	
upper	72.7		77.3	
Income				
under $10,000	69.7	p = ns	80.0	p = ns
$10,000–$19,999	74.1		82.7	
$20,000–$34,999	76.8		81.4	
$35,000+	72.8		79.4	
Subjective Class				
lower	70.2	p = ns	83.9	p = ns
working	73.8		82.3	
middle-upper	71.5		79.9	

Table 3.10   *(continued)*

COMMUNISM (100 = ANTI-COMMUNIST)				
	BLACK		WHITE	
Class Mobility				
stayed same	71.4	p = ns	82.9	p = ns
up 1 quad	75.5		82.3	
up 2–3 quads	74.7		78.4	

1984 VOTE - (100% = REAGAN)				
	BLACK		WHITE	
Education				
less hs	12.6%	p = ns	53.7%	p = .004
hs grad	16.3		65.7	
some college	7.1		73.8	
col grad	11.3		66.1	
Occupational Prestige				
lower	10.1	p = ns	59.6	p = ns
low-mid	14.1		64.6	
mid-upper	10.9		62.7	
upper	11.5		70.8	
Income				
under $10,000	13.2	p = ns	54.0	p = .03
$10,000–$19,999	7.2		63.0	
$20,000–$34,999	13.6		63.1	
$35,000+	17.0		70.2	
Subjective Class				
lower	13.8	p = ns	50.0	p = .03
working	13.0		61.5	
middle-upper	11.4		68.6	
Class Mobility				
stayed same	12.0	p = ns	65.5	p = ns
up 1 quad	15.2		69.0	
up 2–3 quads	9.1		66.9	

Mondale. Thus, in white America class is at least modestly related to partisan vote choice in presidential elections, with upper-class respondents tending to vote for the right-of-center candidate and lower-class respondents the center-left candidate. Class in the black community, however, has hardly any import for presidential choice. Middle- to upper-class blacks do not vote egocentrically on the basis of their presumed, objective class interests; rather, they appear to vote sociotropically, in terms of what they perceive to be the interest of their racial reference group and/or the interest of the nation as a whole.[23] Nor do lower-class blacks translate their relatively more conservative opinions on social issues into votes for socially conservative presidential candidates. These findings point to a simple but often ignored fact of contemporary Afro-American life: Class is essentially irrelevant in the dynamics of partisan political choice in the United States.

Overall, then, liberalism in the black community in the economic, foreign policy, and presidential voting preference arenas appears to be a characteristic of the political culture that distinguishes mainstream black America from the white mainstream. On the social issues black and white attitude differences (where the former may appear more conservative on abortion, the place of women, homosexuality, and civil liberties) appear to be largely the effects of class or are overshadowed by the effects of class. Where this is not the case—school prayer and, to an extent, aspects of the crime issue—it is perhaps a function, in the case of the former, of the value of religiosity in black culture, and in the latter, of the dilemma of being black in a racist social structure, which makes blacks in the United States the victims of both criminals and the criminal justice system.[24] Finally, as we have suggested elsewhere (Seltzer and Smith, 1985:105), analysis of the data on class, class mobility, and ideological inclinations in the black community provides little support for the idea that the college educated, high income middle-class black might constitute the basis for an emerging conservative constituency. Instead, to the extent that there is any class basis for conservatism, it is to be found among the less-educated poor, who tend to be somewhat more conservative on both economic and sociocultural issues.

Conclusion

Class does pattern and structure opinion in the United States, but there is also a significant racial residual, which suggests the possibility of the existence of a relatively distinct Afro-American mass culture that cuts across class lines as it manifests itself in mass opinion. Put another way, class plays a much more significant role in structuring mass opinion in the white community than it does in the black.

We have in this analysis isolated three clusters or subsets of opinions within the larger configuration of American mass culture: class, the ethclass subset, and race.[25] There is a distinctive class ethos or culture in the United States that separates the middle and upper classes from the poor and working classes, and aspects of this class culture are shared by both blacks and whites. For example, middle- to upper-class Americans, black or white, tend to be less alienated (by most measures), more knowledgeable, more interested in politics, more politically efficacious, and more politically involved organizationally and in terms of lobbying and electoral activism. In this limited sense the civic culture in the United States is a middle-class phenomenon. There is also a clear tendency on many of the social issues for middle-class persons to be more liberal and civil libertarian in attitudinal predispositions, and this tendency cuts across race lines in order to constitute an element of class culture. Beyond these opinion elements—principally alienation, civic attitudes and behavior, and traditional or nontraditional attitudes toward such things as the role of women, abortion, homosexuality, and tolerance of deviant ideas, groups, and lifestyles—there is not much that distinguishes the upper-middle and lower classes insofar as mass opinion. Observed racial differences on these opinions, therefore, are not ethnic-cultural in character; rather, they are ethclass phenomena, a by-product of the disproportionate concentration of blacks in the lower class that should wither away as the class structure of blacks comes to resemble more that of whites.[26]

In the white community there tends to be a working class basis for elements of economic opinion and attitudes toward communism, with working-class whites being more liberal on the former (favoring government income redistributionist policies) and more conservative on the latter (more hostile toward communism). Among blacks few statistically significant differences are observed on the economic policy issues (and when they are, class operates in the opposite direction from whites, i.e., it is the black working class that is more conservative) and on communism, middle- and lower-class blacks share essentially the same hostile attitudes, although not as hostile as white Americans.

There thus emerges a third cluster of opinion differences in the United States in addition to class and ethclass, and that is race-specific black cultural opinions. As noted, black Americans across class lines are more liberal on economic policy matters, in support for government spending programs for social betterment, and in attitudes toward military spending and communism. In addition to these manifestations in mass opinion of an Afro-American political subculture, blacks are also more alienated in the interpersonal meaning of the concept and more religious; these are expected cultural differences between the races, given what we know from historical and more recent anthropological field work on the Afro-American community. What effect, if any, these cultural differences have on black political thought and behavior is the question we take up in chapter 5, but first a closer look, beyond class, at the sources of Afro-American opinion formation.

Chapter Four

The Internal Foundations of Afro-American Mass Culture

This is a study in Afro-American mass opinion. Our theoretical approach required us at the outset, however, to employ the race differences paradigm in order to test for the effects of class and ethclass in the formation of the phenomenon in the United States today. Having established the place of class and ethclass in the foundations of Afro-American mass opinion and identified significant observed subcultural residues remaining after the introduction of controls for social class, in this chapter we move beyond class and the race differences paradigm to more detailed study of the internal dynamics of black opinion formation. We analyze the internals of black opinion in terms of such important community differences as gender, age, region, residence, and marital status. In chapter 5 we turn to detailed analysis of the interaction of opinion clusters in the community and their effects on political behavior and ideology.

Moving away from the race differences paradigm insofar as the demographic variables are concerned is useful in the study of minority group opinion and politics (oppressed minorities, that is—blacks, Chicanos, Puerto Ricans, and the native peoples) in the United States for at least two reasons. First, given the rather large structural asymmetries between racial minorities and the white majority in terms of class, status, and power, and having dealt at the outset with the theoretical arguments regarding class as an explanation of interracial differences, it becomes like comparing atheoretical apples and oranges to continue this line of analysis with respect to demographic differences between

the races. That is, there is little in the theoretical or empirical literature on ethnic or racial group differences to suggest that we
should entertain hypotheses that mass opinion differences
between blacks and whites hinge significantly on variables such
as age, gender, or residence, with the possible exception of
region.[1]

Second, as Gordon and Rollock suggest in their 1987 paper
"Communicentric Frames of References in the Pursuit of Scholarship," given the uneven state of our knowledge of minority
groups' attitudes and behavior, knowledge is probably best
advanced at this stage by detailed intragroup minority comparison or contrast.[2] This point is also implicit throughout Walton's
(1985) critique of the extant behavioral literature on blacks and
was suggested by Mack Jones in personal communications back
in 1986. Thus, there appears to be an emergent view among students of Afro-American society and politics that the phenomena
ought to be studied in their own right unless there is some com-
pelling theoretical or policy reason to do otherwise. In this work
we have no such reasons to compare blacks and whites of similar demographic backgrounds in order to understand and
explain Afro-American mass opinion. Thus, we shall devote the
remainder of the book to Afro-American mass opinion itself.

Religiosity

There is a small body of literature that attempts to trace out
the demographic bases or sources of religiosity in the Afro-
American community. A fairly consistent pattern is found—
women, older persons, those with more education and those
born or residing in the South have been found to be more religious (Nelson and Nelson, 1975; Taylor, forthcoming; Taylor,
Thornton, and Chatters, 1987). The data displayed in Table 4.1
confirm the findings of the extant research on the demographic
basis of black religious formation: Women, older persons, and
persons born in the South or currently living in the South are
more religious than others in the black community. In addition,
respondents who are married or have been married exhibit a tendency toward greater religiosity than persons who have never
been married. In two categories where one might have expected
to observe differences in degree of religiosity—type of city and
religious denomination—none are observed. First, it has long
been held that religious commitment and faith in black America

Table 4.1 Intra-Racial Differences Among Blacks—Religiosity

RELIGIOSITY (100 = HIGH RELIGIOSITY)

Sex		
male	54.8	p = .0000
female	66.4	
Age		
18–24	50.9	p = .0000
25–54	59.2	
55+	73.7	
Marital Status7		
married	61.8	p = .01
div/sep	63.0	
never married	54.2	
Region3		
non-South	55.9	p = .0002
South	64.2	
born S, live non-S	69.0	
Type of City		
1–12 SMSA	61.2	p = ns
other large SMSA	63.7	
suburb	65.5	
other urban	61.5	
rural	66.0	
Religion		
Baptist-Methodist	60.9	p = ns
other	64.8	

Guide to Tables in Chapter 4

P-values are reported for demographic differences if they are statistically significant (p < .05) or are of borderline significance (p > .10 < .05).

If a significant demographic effect disappears after controlling for another variable, a number is placed in superscript next to the name of the variable that is no longer significant. The number in superscript refers to which variable causes the demographic difference to disappear. A guide to these numbers is given below:

1. education
2. occupational prestige
3. income
4. subjective class
5. class mobility
6. sex
7. age
8. marital status
9. region
10. type of city
11. religion
12. religiosity

have their roots in the traditional communities of the rural South and tend to attenuate progressively as one moves from rural areas to large cities, where the weight of tradition is less and the overall environment is more secular. Yet no such pattern is observed. Southern blacks do indicate that they are more religious, but beyond that place of residence—big cities, smaller cities, suburbs, or rural areas of the South (virtually all blacks in the United States and in the GSS who live in rural areas live in the South)—is not statistically significant in determining the extent of religiosity. Neither is religious denomination. One might have hypothesized that adherents of the more traditional, fundamentalist faiths—Baptist and Methodist—would exhibit higher levels of religiosity than other, more cosmopolitan religious denominations of blacks, but the differences (65 vs. 61) are not statistically significant.

To the extent that a relatively higher degree of religiosity is, as we contend the data here show, an Afro-American cultural trait that distinguishes mainstream black culture, one would expect that women and the elderly would be more religious. This is so because studies of ethnic cultures in the United States have shown that among all groups it is women and the elderly who are most attuned to and likely to carry forward in the socialization process the core values of the ethnic culture (see the studies of ethnic families in Mindel and Habenstein, 1976). Similarly, as we alluded to earlier, the South is the traditional hard core "Bible Belt" of the United States; thus, it is to be expected that Southerners and persons reared in the region would exhibit this regional cultural variation. And this the data show quite convincingly, females are 12 points more religious than males, persons over 55 are 23 points in excess of those 18-24 and Southerners are 8 to 13 points higher on the scale than persons reared or living in other parts of the country. Looking at these differential bases of the black religious formation in another way, the mean religiosity score for blacks is 62; black males score 7 points less than the community norm, younger blacks, 11 points lower, and non-Southern blacks, six. Finally, it is interesting to note that among blacks, marriage, even if they divorce or separate, tends to predispose individuals toward greater religiosity. However, when we control for age, this difference disappears, suggesting that it might be an artifact of the greater religiosity of the middle-aged and elderly, who are more likely to be married, separated, or divorced.

What is clear here in terms of the sources of black religiosity is consistent with past findings and in the direction students of ethnic cultures would expect. Older persons, women, and persons socialized in the traditional geographic culture—"down home" in the Afro-American experience—are more likely to adhere to this core cultural residue.

Alienation

What is to be expected insofar as demographic patterns in terms of the various dimensions or measurements of alienation? The extant literature is not very helpful, in that there is no consistent pattern in the findings in terms of the demographic correlates of alienation in the black community. Most studies have found relatively few statistically significant intraracial differences among blacks after controlling for social class (variously measured), although there are reports that younger blacks may be more alienated or dissatisfied on some dimensions (Hughes and Thomas, 1986) and that Southerners may be less alienated than non-Southern blacks (Aberbach and Walker, 1970a). Yet overall the empirical literature on the problem is either silent or shows little difference beyond class.

Theoretically, one might hypothesize that black women would be more alienated than black men—indeed, the most alienated segment of the American population taken as a whole, given what some refer to as their "triple oppression" based on class, race, and gender (see Lewis, 1977; Malveaux, 1987; Davis, 1981). Or, given the region's relatively higher degree historically of class and race oppression, we might expect Southern blacks to be more alienated. Yet, given the role of religiosity in Southern black life one might entertain an alternative hypothesis, since on some dimensions of alienation Southern blacks and those active in the church have been found to be less alienated (Aberbach and Walker, 1970a:1203). Similarly, one might guess that persons residing in the anomic isolation of the nation's huge cities might be more alienated on some dimensions than suburban or rural residents. Although some studies show a tendency for young blacks to be more alienated than the middle-aged and elderly, one might hypothesize the opposite, since in the post-civil rights era their life chances in the United States might be (or at least perceived to be) better.

The results in Table 4.2 do not provide strong or consistent support across the three dimensions of alienation for any of these theoretical speculations. On the satisfaction dimension there is a tendency for married persons[3] and persons in rural areas to be less alienated than singles or persons living in urban areas, and on the index of general alienation there is a tendency for black women to be more alienated than men. But generally, relatively few demographic differences are observed in the incidence of alienation in the black community. On most dimensions of the

Table 4.2 Intra-Racial Differences Among Blacks—Alienation

SATISFACTION (100 = HIGH DISSATISFACTION)

Sex		
male	40.5	p = ns
female	40.3	
Age		
18–24	42.1	p = ns
25–54	41.1	
55+	38.0	
Marital Status3		
married	37.5	p = .005
div/sep	43.6	
never married	42.2	
Region		
non-South	39.9	p = ns
South	40.6	
born S, live non-S	40.7	
Type of City		
1–12 SMSA	39.9	p = .07
other large SMSA	41.6	
suburb	34.9	
other urban	41.2	
rural	38.9	
Religion		
Baptist-Methodist	40.1	p = ns
other	40.9	

GENERAL ALIENATION (100 = HIGH ALIENATION)

Sex		
male	60.0	p = .006
female	68.7	
Age		
18–24	65.8	p = ns
25–54	65.9	
55+	64.0	
Marital Status		
married	65.2	p = ns
div/sep	64.9	
never married	64.9	
Region		
non-South	67.1	p = ns
South	65.9	
born S, live non-S	60.1	

Table 4.2   *(continued)*

GENERAL ALIENATION (100 = HIGH ALIENATION)

Type of City

1-12 SMSA	62.5	p = ns
other large SMSA	69.3	
suburb	61.5	
other urban	67.3	
rural	57.9	

Religion

Baptist-Methodist	65.7	p = ns
other	64.7	

INTERPERSONAL ALIENATION (100 = HIGH ALIENATION)

Sex

male	71.4	p = ns
female	72.9	

Age

18–24	72.8	p = ns
25–54	72.8	
55+	71.0	

Marital Status

married	72.9	p = ns
div/sep	73.2	
never married	71.8	

Region

non-South	71.8	p = ns
South	72.6	
born S, live non-S	72.7	

Type of City

1-12 SMSA	74.6	p = ns
other large SMSA	66.7	
suburb	74.0	
other urban	71.6	
rural	77.0	

Religion

Baptist-Methodist	71.8	p = ns
other	73.2	

concept the young and the old, the married and unmarried, Southerners and non-Southerners, city dwellers, suburbanites, and country folk exhibit the same relatively high degree of alienation. On interpersonal alienation—the relative suspiciousness of others—which we identified earlier as one of the distinguishing features of Afro-American culture, each demographic category exhibits roughly the same high scores, from the low to mid seventies. The stability of the scores across segments of the black community is remarkable, indicating a high degree of cohesiveness on this cultural trait.

The Civic Culture

Civic attitudes in black America are to some extent shaped by demographic characteristics, but as the data reported in Table 4.3 show, there are more similarities than differences among black Americans along these dimensions except for political knowledge.

Table 4.3   Intra-Racial Differences Among Blacks in Civic Attitudes

POLITICAL KNOWLEDGE (100 = HIGH KNOWLEDGE)		
Sex[1]		
male	43.3	p = .03
female	37.0	
Age		
18–24	28.0	p = .004
25–54	41.9	
55+	40.1	
Marital Status[7]		
married	42.8	p = .008
div/sep	43.7	
never married	33.3	
Region[10]		
non-South	44.0	p = .004
South	34.7	
born S, live non-S	44.2	
Type of City		
1–12 SMSA	51.7	p = .0000
other large SMSA	41.3	
suburb	34.9	
other urban	31.2	
rural	45.6	
Religion		
Baptist-Methodist	40.9	p = ns
other	37.0	

POLITICAL INTEREST (100 = LOW INTEREST)		
Sex		
male	38.7	p = .0000
female	51.7	

Table 4.3 *(continued)*

POLITICAL INTEREST (100 = LOW INTEREST)

Age
18–24	53.1	p = ns
25–54	44.9	
55+	47.2	

Marital Status
married	44.1	p = ns
div/sep	46.2	
never married	47.9	

Region
non-South	44.2	p = ns
South	48.9	
born S, live non-S	45.5	

Type of City
1–12 SMSA	43.6	p = ns
other large SMSA	50.3	
suburb	42.5	
other urban	46.0	
rural	55.5	

Religion
Baptist-Methodist	45.0	p = ns
other	49.4	

POLITICAL EFFICACY (100 = LOW EFFICACY)

Sex
male	45.4	p = ns
female	47.9	

Age
18–24	46.7	p = ns
25–54	46.1	
55+	48.7	

Marital Status
married	46.3	p = ns
div/sep	45.6	
never married	45.7	

Region[1]
non-South	42.8	p = .02
South	50.0	
born S, live non-S	47.1	

Type of City
1–12 SMSA	45.1	p = ns
other large SMSA	49.3	
suburb	40.7	
other urban	49.0	
rural	48.5	

Religion
Baptist-Methodist	47.0	p = ns
other	46.5	

Table 4.3   *(continued)*

POLITICAL TRUST (100 = HIGH DISTRUST)		
Sex		
male	64.6	p = ns
female	66.9	
Age		
18–24	61.4	p = ns
25–54	66.8	
55+	66.6	
Marital Status		
married	64.0	p = ns
div/sep	67.1	
never married	65.5	
Region[10]		
non-South	69.5	p = .0000
South	61.4	
born S, live non-S	71.8	
Type of City		
1–12 SMSA	73.2	p = .0000
other large SMSA	67.7	
suburb	56.6	
other urban	66.0	
rural	53.3	
Religion		
Baptist-Methodist	65.0	p = ns
other	67.8	

    Region and place of residence are the critical cleavages in the distribution of civic attitudes in black America. Black Americans who live outside the South[4] and in large cities tend to be more knowledgeable and efficacious, but also more alienated or distrustful of political authority. Thus, Northern big-city black mass opinion, in contrast to its rural Southern counterpart, tends to be more informed about politics and is more politically efficacious, yet it is also more cynical about the political system. This regional cleavage in attitude patterns is consistent with that observed 20 years ago during the crest of the black power rebellion (Aberbach and Walker, 1970b; Mitchell, Brown, and Raine, 1973). Apart from this regional effect, gender, age, and marital status do not shape civic attitudes, except on political knowledge and political interest. Women,[5] the very young, and single persons[6] demonstrated less knowledge about politics, and women had less interest in politics than men. This pattern is not unusual; in most communities young people, women, and single persons have tended to be less interested in and knowledgeable about political issues and personalities.

In Table 4.4 data on organizational behavior are shown. A tendency is observed for males and especially suburban residents (who score 10 points higher than persons residing elsewhere) to report organizational membership, and suburban blacks are much more likely to report membership in political organizations. Suburban residents and the middle-aged are also more active in organizations than other demographic segments of the community. The most interesting finding is the absence of a region cleavage and the saliency of the suburban factor in enhancing this form of political behavior among blacks.

Table 4.4 Intra-Racial Differences Among Blacks—Organizational Behavior

MEMBERSHIP IN ORGANIZATIONS (100 = HIGH MEMBERSHIP)

Sex		
male	15.5	p = .06
female	12.5	
Age		
18–24	13.6	p = ns
25–54	14.8	
55+	11.4	
Marital Status		
married	15.6	p = ns
div/sep	15.4	
never married	12.0	
Region		
non-South	14.5	p = ns
South	13.6	
born S, live non-S	12.4	
Type of City		
1–12 SMSA	13.0	p = .0005
other large SMSA	12.3	
suburb	23.3	
other urban	12.5	
rural	11.3	
Religion		
Baptist-Methodist	12.9	p = ns
other	15.3	

MEMBERSHIP IN POLITICAL ORGANIZATIONS (100 = HIGH MEMBERSHIP)

Sex		
male	16.0	p = ns
female	13.3	
Age		
18–24	13.9	p = ns
25–54	15.7	
55+	11.3	

Table 4.4   *(continued)*

Marital Status
married	15.2	p = ns
div/sep	16.9	
never married	12.8	

Region
non-South	14.9	p = ns
South	14.4	
born S, live non-S	11.7	

Type of City
1–12 SMSA	13.1	p = .0001
other large SMSA	12.7	
suburb	26.5	
other urban	12.3	
rural	12.0	

Religion
Baptist-Methodist	13.4	p = ns
other	15.9	

ACTIVE IN ORGANIZATIONS (100 = HIGH ACTIVITY)

Sex
male	14.1	p = ns
female	13.1	

Age
18–24	10.9	p = .08
25–54	15.2	
55+	11.2	

Marital Status
married	14.2	p = ns
div/sep	16.9	
never married	11.4	

Region
non-South	14.1	p = ns
South	13.5	
born S, live non-S	12.1	

Type of City
1–12 SMSA	11.3	p = .0004
other large SMSA	11.8	
suburb	24.8	
other urban	12.0	
rural	13.5	

Religion
Baptist-Methodist	13.1	p = ns
other	14.3	

Table 4.4 *(continued)*

LEADERSHIP IN ORGANIZATIONS (100 = HIGH PARTICIPATION)

Sex		
male	24.9	p = ns
female	25.6	
Age		
18–24	19.1	p = ns
25–54	26.0	
55+	26.9	
Marital Status[12]		
married	28.4	p = .01
div/sep	27.8	
never married	19.7	
Region		
non-South	25.1	p = ns
South	25.5	
born S, live non-S	25.3	
Type of City		
1–12 SMSA	25.6	p = ns
other large SMSA	26.9	
suburb	32.6	
other urban	23.0	
rural	25.1	
Religion		
Baptist-Methodist	25.6	p = ns
other	25.2	

In terms of lobbying, problem-solving activities, electoral activism, and voting (see Table 4.5), to the extent that intraracial differences among blacks exist the tendency is for males, middle aged and married respondents to report somewhat higher levels of participation. But in general the differences, although statistically significant, are not striking; what is perhaps most interesting is the absence of the regional cleavage observed in earlier studies, especially in terms of lobbying and electoral activism (see Nie and Verba, 1972:170–71), indicating that Southern Afro-American civic culture is now about as participant as that of other parts of the country. There is still a regional cleavage in voting at both the local and presidential levels, with Southern and rural blacks less likely to vote than Northern and urban citizens. This region gap is not a function, like many other regional effects, of the relatively lower social class positions of Southern and rural blacks, but is probably an effect of the legacy of blatant systemic discrimination in access to the ballot. The huge age gap in voting is not at all surprising, since everywhere the young tend to vote less; voter registration activists in the black community have long targeted the 18–24 age group as the largest pool of unregistered black voters (Reid, 1981).

Table 4.5   Intra-Racial Differences Among Blacks—Civic Participation

---

LOBBYING (100 = HIGH LOBBYING)

Sex		
male	21.7	p = ns
female	19.0	
Age[3]		
18–24	11.8	p = .05
25–54	22.3	
55+	19.4	
Marital Status		
married	23.7	p = .07
div/sep	23.9	
never married	15.8	
Region		
non-South	21.9	p = ns
South	18.5	
born S, live non-S	20.8	
Type of City		
1–12 SMSA	22.8	p = ns
other large SMSA	21.5	
suburb	27.0	
other urban	15.7	
rural	21.1	
Religion		
Baptist-Methodist	18.3	p = ns
other	23.3	

PROBLEM SOLVING (100 = HIGH ACTIVITY)

Sex		
male	24.5	p = ns
female	23.1	
Age[3,8]		
18–24	13.8	p = .04
25–54	25.1	
55+	25.5	
Marital Status[7]		
married	22.5	p = .02
div/sep	31.0	
never married	19.9	

PROBLEM SOLVING (100 = HIGH ACTIVITY)

Region		
non-South	24.6	p = ns
South	21.8	
born S, live non-S	27.0	

Table 4.5 *(continued)*

PROBLEM SOLVING (100 = HIGH ACTIVITY)

Type of City
1–12 SMSA	27.6	p = ns
other large SMSA	24.8	
suburb	27.0	
other urban	20.8	
rural	23.7	

Religion
Baptist-Methodist	25.3	p = ns
other	20.2	

ELECTORAL ACTIVISM (100 = HIGH PARTICIPATION)

Sex
male	23.6	p = .005
female	17.1	

Age[3]
18–24	15.1	p = .005
25–54	22.8	
55+	15.6	

Marital Status
married	20.1	p = ns
div/sep	21.8	
never married	19.3	

Region
non-South	21.8	p = ns
South	18.1	
born S, live non-S	19.7	

Type of City
1–12 SMSA	25.6	p = .005
other large SMSA	17.5	
suburb	25.8	
other urban	15.4	
rural	17.8	

Religion
Baptist-Methodist	19.2	p = ns
other	20.5	

VOTED IN 1984 PRESIDENTIAL ELECTION (100% = YES)

Sex
male	62.7	p = ns
female	65.7	

Age
18–24	39.1	p = .0000
25–54	61.5	
55+	78.1	

Table 4.5   *(continued)*

VOTED IN 1984 PRESIDENTIAL ELECTION (100% = YES)

Marital Status[7]		
married	67.5	p = .03
div/sep	67.5	
never married	54.0	
Region		
non-South	69.2	p = .0007
South	56.8	
born S, live non-S	77.9	
Type of City		
1–12 SMSA	73.0	p = .0001
other large SMSA	74.2	
suburb	67.3	
other urban	48.6	
rural	66.7	
Religion		
Baptist-Methodist	66.7	p = ns
other	60.5	

VOTE IN LOCAL ELECTIONS (100 = FREQUENT VOTING)

Sex		
male	55.7	p = ns
female	55.5	
Age		
18–24	30.6	p = .0000
25–54	53.4	
55+	72.4	
Marital Status[7]		
married	60.0	p = .0002
div/sep	58.4	
never married	43.8	
Region		
non-South	56.0	p = .0000
South	48.4	
born S, live non-S	76.1	
Type of City		
1–12 SMSA	64.0	p = .0002
other large SMSA	62.7	
suburb	49.4	
other urban	45.9	
rural	56.1	
Religion[7]		
Baptist-Methodist	58.2	p = .03
other	50.7	

It is somewhat surprising not to find a gender gap in voting (the differences at the presidential level—66 percent female and

63 percent male) are not statistically significant, given that studies of the 1984 election found that black women voted at a rate 7.5 percent higher than men (Cavanagh, 1985:16); several scholars have pointed to gender as an emergent cleavage in black voter participation (see Williams and Harris, 1987, for example). And given our previous findings on suburban organizational participation we might also have expected to observe differences in voting; instead, there are either no statistically significant differences or they are modest.

Overall, then, the civic culture in the black community is shaped at the attitudinal level by region and place of residence, with Northern and big-city mass opinion being both more civic and more cynical. Organizational membership and activism tend to predominate among males, the middle-aged and suburban residents, whereas other participant behavior—lobbying, problem solving, and electoral activism—tends to be structured by gender, age, and marital status, with no significant region or place of residence cleavages. Region does continue to form an important basis of voting behavior, along with age. Yet these region and residential formations in Afro-American mass opinion, although important, should not obscure the rather high degree of sameness across demographic categories in the Afro-American civic culture.

Ideology

Although there have been in recent years a good number of studies investigating the relationship between class cleavages and ideology in black America, hardly any studies have been done of other possible sources of ideological differences among black Americans. As we found in this study, most other works on class and ideology in black America have found weak or nonexistent relationships. We expect, however, that the unexplored sources of black opinion formation—age, gender, region, marital status—are more likely to reveal significant ideological cleavages, especially on the social issues so important to family and community life.

In Table 4.6 we first report the results on self-identified ideology and the economic dimension of the concept. Three effects are observed on self-identification: The young and elderly persons identify themselves as conservative more than do persons living in rural areas. The middle-score of young blacks (49) on the conservative-liberalism index is somewhat surprising, since young people usually are somewhat more liberal than others, but this finding is not inconsistent with recent studies that show younger blacks identify less strongly with the relatively more liberal Democratic party and are more likely to identify with the more conservative Republicans (Cavanagh, 1985:37; see also McCormick, Thornton, and Hill, 1988).[7] Except for age and residence, no other demographic effects are observed for ideological self-identification.

Table 4.6   Intra-Racial Differences Among Blacks—Self-Identified Ideology and Economic Policy Preferences

IDEOLOGICAL SELF-IDENTIFICATION (100 = CONSERVATIVE)

Sex		
male	44.8	p = ns
female	45.9	
Age		
18–24	49.5	p = .01
25–54	42.7	
55+	49.6	
Marital Status		
married	46.3	p = ns
div/sep	42.8	
never married	45.8	
Region		
non-South	42.6	p = ns
South	47.9	
born S, live non-S	45.6	
Type of City[a]		
1–12 SMSA	41.4	p = .04
other large SMSA	42.9	
suburb	45.3	
other urban	49.3	
rural	53.6	
Religion		
Baptist-Methodist	45.4	p = ns
other	45.6	

SPENDING ON SOCIAL PROGRAMS (100 = SPEND LESS)

Sex		
male	21.6	p = ns
female	19.3	
Age		
18–24	20.0	p = ns
25–54	19.6	
55+	22.0	
Marital Status		
married	21.9	p = ns
div/sep	20.6	
never married	18.7	

Table 4.6 *(continued)*

SPENDING ON SOCIAL PROGRAMS (100 = SPEND LESS)

Region[10]

non-South	17.5	p = .002
South	23.3	
born S, live non-S	17.6	

Type of City

1–12 SMSA	14.7	p = .0001
other large SMSA	21.4	
suburb	21.9	
other urban	24.0	
rural	20.1	

Religion

Baptist-Methodist	20.4	p = ns
other	20.1	

GOVERNMENT REDISTRIBUTE INCOME (100 = CONSERVATIVE)

Sex

male	31.6	p = ns
female	30.9	

Age

18–24	29.2	p = .02
25–54	34.2	
55+	25.7	

Marital Status

married	32.7	p = ns
div/sep	30.1	
never married	31.6	

Region

non-South	26.7	p = .0003
South	36.7	
born S, live non-S	24.7	

Type of City[9]

1–12 SMSA	26.3	p = .03
other large SMSA	34.2	
suburb	34.0	
other urban	29.1	
rural	43.4	

Religion

Baptist-Methodist	29.0	p = .02
other	35.4	

GOVERNMENT HELP POOR/SICK (100 = CONSERVATIVE)

Sex

male	30.2	p = ns
female	28.1	

Table 4.6   *(continued)*

GOVERNMENT HELP POOR/SICK (100 = CONSERVATIVE)

Age		
18–24	30.4	p = ns
25–54	29.3	
55+	27.3	
Marital Status		
married	31.6	p = ns
div/sep	26.5	
never married	30.1	
Region[10]		
non-South	25.4	p = .0000
South	34.2	
born S, live non-S	21.3	
Type of City		
1–12 SMSA	21.3	p = .0000
other large SMSA	33.8	
suburb	27.2	
other urban	28.9	
rural	47.8	
Religion		
Bapist-Methodist	29.2	p = ns
other	28.7	

There is an even higher degree of homogeneity among blacks in terms of support for government spending on domestic social programs. Southerners[8] and respondents living outside the largest metropolitan areas are somewhat less supportive of government spending on domestic programs than other blacks, but even here the average score on the index is only 20. On support for government programs to redistribute income Southerners, middle-aged persons, and rural residents[9] tend to be less liberal; on the issue of government programs to help the poor and sick the age effect does not occur, but region[10] and residence remain. Thus, in general, conservatism on economic matters, to the degree that it exists among blacks, tends to be anchored in the South, especially the rural South, where on some issues—redistribution of income and government assistance to the poor and sick—rural black Southerners favor less government spending compared to other categories of black Americans.[11] Region thus appears again to be a critical cleavage or determinant in Afro-American opinion formation.

The demographic basis of social issue opinion formation among blacks is first shown in Table 4.7. On abortion, no gender effects are present, but strong region and age effects are clear. Elderly persons, respondents born in the South, and rural resi-

Table 4.7 Intra-Racial Attitudes Among Blacks - Social Issues

ABORTION (100 = PRO-ABORTION)

Sex
male	49.1	p = ns
female	50.2	

Age
18–24	61.4	p = .0000
25–54	53.1	
55+	37.5	

Marital Status
married	48.7	p = .07
div/sep	50.1	
never married	56.9	

Region
non-South	58.8	p = .0000
South	46.0	
born S, live non-S	42.0	

Type of City [3]
1–12 SMSA	52.7	p = .01
other large SMSA	52.6	
suburb	55.0	
other urban	43.7	
rural	37.2	

Religion
Baptist-Methodist	50.6	p = ns
other	48.7	

PREMARITAL SEX (% ALWAYS WRONG)

Sex
male	19.7%	p = .0002
female	35.6	

Age [9,12]
18–24	22.9	p = .03
25–54	26.9	
55+	38.7	

Marital Status [9]
married	28.4	p = .03
div/sep	32.2	
never married	18.0	

Region
non-South	18.0	p = .0001
South	37.4	
born S, live non-S	26.3	

Type of City [9,11]
1–12 SMSA	20.5	p = .007
other large SMSA	7.3	
suburb	25.6	
other urban	37.4	
rural	45.1	

Table 4.7   *(continued)*

Premarital Sex (% always wrong)

Religion
Baptist-Methodist	29.7	p = ns
other	28.7	

Extramarital Sex (% always wrong)

Sex
male	62.5%	p = .001
female	75.9	

Age
18–24	6.9	p = .07
25–54	67.6	
55+	78.1	

Marital Status
married	75.9	p = .09
div/sep	65.6	
never married	66.4	

Region
non-South	63.9	p = .009
South	77.0	
born S, live non-S	67.0	

Type of City[12]
1–12 SMSA	60.0	p = .02
other large SMSA	73.1	
suburb	79.7	
other urban	74.3	
rural	80.6	

Religion
Baptist-Methodist	69.6	p = ns
other	72.8	

Homosexuality (% always wrong)

Sex
male	84.6%	p = ns
female	85.9	

Age
18–24	78.4	p = ns
25–54	85.9	
55+	87.8	

Marital Status
married	89.9	
div/sep	83.7	
never married	81.9	p = ns

Region[12]
non-South	79.5	p = .02
South	87.6	
born S, live non-S	90.6	

Table 4.7 *(continued)*

HOMOSEXUALITY (% ALWAYS WRONG)

Type of City[12]

1–12 SMSA	77.6	p = .03
other large SMSA	88.5	
suburb	83.3	
other urban	86.1	
rural	97.2	

Religion

Baptist-Methodist	85.6	p = ns
other	84.9	

WOMEN TAKE CARE OF HOME NOT COUNTRY (% AGREE)

Sex

male	37.5%	p = ns
female	31.4	

Age[1]

18–24	27.9	p = .0001
25–54	28.2	
55+	48.5	

Marital Status

married	34.0	p = ns
div/sep	26.9	
never married	27.8	

Region

non-South	21.1	p = .0002
South	40.5	
born S, live non-S	37.8	

Type of City

1–12 SMSA	25.2	p = .0000
other large SMSA	40.6	
suburb	35.1	
other urban	26.4	
rural	62.7	

Religion

Baptist-Methodist	34.7	p = ns
other	32.0	

MARRIED WOMEN SHOULD NOT WORK (% AGREE)

Sex

male	27.6%	p = ns
female	29.8	

Age

18–24	24.6	p = .0001
25–54	23.2	
55+	43.7	

Table 4.7   *(continued)*

MARRIED WOMEN SHOULD NOT WORK (% AGREE)

Marital Status		
married	27.5	p = ns
div/sep	29.3	
never married	24.0	
Region[10]		
non-South	18.4	p = .001
South	35.2	
born S, live non-S	31.0	
Type of City		
1–12 SMSA	23.0	p = .0003
other large SMSA	36.4	
suburb	22.9	
other urban	24.5	
rural	54.0	
Religion		
Baptist-Methodist	29.2	p = ns
other	28.6	

dents[12] are more conservative. For example, rural Southerners and the elderly score about 30 on the abortion index, compared to about 50 among the other demographic groups. A slight tendency is also observed for single, never married persons to be more accepting of abortion.

On other issues involving sexual intimacy and the rights of women a more complex pattern of opinion formation is seen. Women, the elderly,[13] the divorced or separated,[14] Southerners, and rural residents[15] are more likely to view premarital sex as always wrong (about a third of each, except rural Southerners, where the percentage is 45 percent, compared to about 20 percent for the other categories). A similar pattern is observed on extramarital sex, where women, the elderly, and rural Southerners are strongly opposed. Opposition to homosexuality in the black community is widespread, but it is most pronounced among elderly rural Southerners (97 percent of rural residents agree that homosexuality is always wrong). The tendency toward a liberal view here is found among the young and residents of large cities. The really salient cleavage on these issues of traditional family or sexual practices is here, as before, region.

On the role of women in society—whether they should be involved in politics and whether married women should work—the same pattern as above is observed. Elderly, Southern, and rural residents tend to be conservative or traditional in their attitudes. It is interesting to observe that there are no statistically significant gender or marital status effects on these attitudes toward the traditional role of women. But again the rural-non-rural cleavage is most striking; more than half of rural respondents do not approve of married women working and nearly two-thirds agree that women should confine themselves to the home and leave running the country to men.

On the issue of crime, the data in Table 4.8 also show interesting gender, age, and region effects on opinion formation. First, women fear crime much more than men (63 percent vs. 24 percent) and people in big cities also report greater fear. Women, non-Southerners, *and* urban residents[16] tend to think the courts are too lenient on persons accused of crimes. Yet on the death penalty these cleavages disappear, with only a slight tendency for married persons to be in favor and rural Southerners to be opposed to what some view as the ultimate means of crime control. Thus, the much greater fear of crime among black women, non-Southerners, and big-city residents does not translate into commensurate support for death as its punishment. Finally, in the crime area legalization of drugs finds greater levels of support among males, young people, and Northern residents, while the elderly, Southerners, and rural residents are strong in their opposition to legal use of marijuana—the most benign of the proscribed drugs.

Finally, in the social issue domain the data in Table 4.9 on civil libertarian attitudes and support for school prayer show the now consistent pattern in internal black opinion formation. The elderly, Southern respondents, and especially rural residents are

Table 4.8 Intra-Racial Attitudes Among Blacks—Crime

FEAR OF CRIME (% FEAR TO WALK)

Sex		
male	23.6%	p = .0000
female	63.2	
Age		
18–24	43.4	p = ns
25–54	45.6	
55+	54.6	
Marital Status		
married	43.2	p = ns
div/sep	52.3	
never married	42.7	
Region		
non-South	42.7	p = ns
South	49.8	
born S, live non-S	52.9	

Table 4.8   *(continued)*

FEAR OF CRIME (% FEAR TO WALK)

Type of City
1–12 SMSA	52.7	p = .02
other large SMSA	56.9	
suburb	41.0	
other urban	40.3	
rural	36.8	

Religion
Baptist-Methodist	48.7	p = ns
other	46.6	

COURTS NOT HARSH ENOUGH (% AGREE)

Sex
male	71.1%	p = .01
female	80.9	

Age
18-24	74.0	p = .08
25-54	74.6	
55+	83.9	

Marital Status
married	79.6	p = ns
div/sep	76.5	
never married	74.5	

Region
non-South	81.5	p = .01
South	71.4	
born S, live non-S	84.3	

Type of City[a]
1–12 SMSA	85.2	p = .007
other large SMSA	80.5	
suburb	75.0	
other urban	66.7	
rural	82.4	

Religion
Baptist-Methodist	77.9	p = ns
other	75.9	

FAVOR DEATH PENALTY (% FAVOR)

Sex
male	44.3%	p = ns
female	50.7	

Age
18–24	44.6	p = ns
25–54	50.5	
55+	45.2	

Table 4.8   *(continued)*

FAVOR DEATH PENALTY (% FAVOR)

Marital Status
married	49.0	p = .05
div/sep	56.6	
never married	41.7	

Region
non-South	50.9	p = ns
South	47.6	
born S, live non-S	43.8	

Type of City
1–12 SMSA	47.7	p = ns
other large SMSA	50.4	
suburb	54.4	
other urban	46.2	
rural	38.7	

Religion
Baptist-Methodist	51.3	p = .10
other	42.9	

NOT LEGALIZE MARIJUANA (% AGREE)

Sex
male	75.5%	p = .0005
female	87.6	

Age
18–24	76.0	p = .001
25–54	80.1	
55+	92.5	

Marital Status
married	85.8	p = ns
div/sep	79.2	
never married	78.6	

Region[12]
non-South	77.9	p = .04
South	84.4	
born S, live non-S	89.4	

Type of City
1–12 SMSA	83.9	p = ns
other large SMSA	82.0	
suburb	78.0	
other urban	84.4	
rural	88.9	

Religion
Baptist-Methodist	83.3	p = ns
other	82.3	

more conservative or less tolerant of deviant ideas and lifestyles and more supportive of state-sponsored prayer in school.

On the two foreign policy measures—attitudes toward communism and defense/space spending—and the vote in the 1984 election, no significant differences are observed with respect to gender, age, region, or residence (see Tables 4.10 and 4.11). The tendency toward a relatively more liberal foreign policy posture and vote in black American mass opinion is a fairly homogeneous attitude set.

Table 4.9   Intra-Racial Attitudes Among Blacks - Civil Liberties and School Prayer

DISAPPROVE SUPREME COURT'S DECISION ON SCHOOL PRAYER
(100 = SUPREME COURT WRONG)

Sex		
male	74.7	p = ns
female	80.9	
Age		
18–24	63.9	p = .003
25–54	78.3	
55+	85.8	
Marital Status		
married	80.5	p = .06
div/sep	80.5	
never married	69.7	
Region[12]		
non-South	70.1	p = .007
South	83.3	
born S, live non-S	79.7	
Type of City		
1–12 SMSA	75.2	p = .01
other large SMSA	77.1	
suburb	94.9	
other urban	77.2	
rural	92.5	
Religion		
Baptist-Methodist	79.2	p = ns
other	77.2	

CIVIL LIBERTIES (ALL QUESTIONS) (100 = ANTI-CIVIL LIBERTIES)

Sex		
male	41.8	p = .06
female	46.3	
Age1		
18–24	44.4	p = .003
25–54	41.4	
55+	50.8	

Table 4.9 *(continued)*

CIVIL LIBERTIES (ALL QUESTIONS) (100 = ANTI-CIVIL LIBERTIES)

Marital Status
married	42.2	p = ns
div/sep	46.4	
never married	43.2	

Region[10,12]
non-South	39.4	p = .005
South	46.4	
born S, live non-S	49.7	

Type of City
1–12 SMSA	37.0	p = .0007
other large SMSA	48.4	
suburb	39.0	
other urban	49.8	
rural	43.9	

CIVIL LIBERTIES (ALL QUESTIONS) (100 = ANTI-CIVIL LIBERTIES)

Religion
Baptist-Methodist	45.5	p = ns
other	43.3	

CIVIL LIBERTIES (EXCLUDING RACIST QUESTIONS) (100 = ANTI-CIVIL LIBERTIES)

Sex
male	40.8	p = ns
female	44.8	

Age[1]
18–24	42.6	p = .002
25–54	40.2	
55+	49.6	

Marital Status
married	41.3	p = ns
div/sep	44.9	
never married	41.7	

Region[1]
non-South	38.3	p = .006
South	45.0	
born S, live non-S	48.3	

Type of City[12]
1-12 SMSA	36.1	p = .0007
other large SMSA	46.9	
suburb	36.7	
other urban	48.3	
rural	45.4	

Religion
Baptist-Methodist	44.0	p = ns
other	42.4	

Table 4.10 Intra-Racial Attitudes Among Blacks—Foreign Policy

SPENDING ON MILITARY AND SPACE (100 = SPEND LESS)

Sex		
male	60.9	p = ns
female	62.9	
Age		
18–24	62.1	p = ns
25–54	60.9	
55+	65.2	
Marital Status		
married	58.6	p = .006
div/sep	67.1	
never married	60.9	
Region		
non-South	63.5	p = .07
South	59.8	
born S, live non-S	65.7	
Type of City		
1–12 SMSA	66.2	p = .07
other large SMSA	59.3	
suburb	63.7	
other urban	62.5	
rural	54.0	
Religion		
Baptist-Methodist	62.0	p = ns
other	62.3	

COMMUNISM (100 = ANTI-COMMUNIST)

Sex		
male	71.2	p = ns
female	73.8	
Age		
18–24	67.5	p = ns
25–54	73.3	
55+	74.6	
Marital Status		
married	74.8	p = ns
div/sep	72.9	
never married	70.5	
Region		
non-South	71.6	p = ns
South	72.9	
born S, live non-S	74.8	
Type of City		
1–12 SMSA	70.5	p = ns
other large SMSA	72.1	
suburb	71.7	
other urban	75.6	
rural	74.3	

Table 4.10 *(continued)*

COMMUNISM (100 = ANTI-COMMUNIST)		
Religion		
Baptist-Methodist	73.6	p = ns
other	71.2	

Table 4.11 Intra-Racial Differences Among Blacks—
Vote for Reagan in 1984

WHO VOTED FOR (% REAGAN)		
Sex		
male	15.2%	p = ns
female	10.6	
Age		
18–24	5.9	p = ns
25–54	15.2	
55+	8.9	
Marital Status		
married	12.7	p = ns
div/sep	8.6	
never married	12.3	
Region		
non-South	9.5	p = .08
South	17.2	
born S, live non-S	7.5	
Type of City		
1–12 SMSA	12.7	p = .10
other large SMSA	8.1	
suburb	16.2	
other urban	10.6	
rural	30.0	
Religion		
Baptist-Methodist	10.2	p = ns
other	17.0	

Conclusion

Clearly, in terms of the internal dynamics of Afro-American mass opinion region is the critical cleavage, more important in some ways than class in shaping the internal formations of Afro-American opinion differences. Southern blacks, especially those residing in rural areas, are much more conservative on both economic and social issues, but especially on many of the latter. This region cleavage is important in understanding the contours of mass opinion in the black community, because more than half

(53 percent) of the black population lives in the South and 20 percent live in the rural areas of the region (U.S. Bureau of the Census, 1983:5). Thus, we are talking about a substantial part of the black community, and it is apparent that the political culture of the Southern region, with its fundamentalist religious ethos and its emphasis on traditional values and lifestyles, results in a more conservative issue stance on economic and social issues.

Suburban blacks are more active organizationally than blacks living elsewhere (approximately one-fifth of blacks live in census-defined suburban areas, see U.S. Bureau of the Census, 1983:5), but significant differences are not observed on ideology or civic attitudes or behavior, although, interestingly, suburban blacks vote less than blacks living elsewhere. Suburbanization in the United States has often been said to foster the development of community and neighborhood organizations—a community of "joiners" (see Gans, 1967, and Jackson, 1972)—and this process seems to be having the same effect on black suburban-ites (on black suburbanization, see Farley, 1970, and Schnore, Andre, and Sharp, 1976). Yet on basic ideological questions and other forms of political behavior (such as lobbying and electoral activism) suburban blacks are not distinguishable from blacks living elsewhere (except, as noted above, in voting behavior), suggesting that blacks in suburbia may become "joiners" like their white counterparts, but stand apart from white suburban-ites in terms of ideology and other elements of the civic culture.

On many economic and social issues residents of the largest twelve cities are more liberal, but aside from region and residence the other important demographic bases of black opinion formation are age and gender. Women tend to be more religious and, on the social issues dealing with sexual intimacy (but not homosexuality) and crime, more conservative. This is not unexpected, but what is a bit surprising is that black women are not more likely than men to hold "liberated" attitudes toward the role of women in society. Finally, the elderly tend to be more conservative on some issues of economic and social policy. Again, no surprise, since in all communities older persons tend to be more religious and conservative or traditional in attitudes, especially on matters of sex and traditional family values.

Overall, then, the internal basis of black mass opinion for-mation is anchored in region and residence. In his inquiry into ghetto culture and community, Hannerz (1969:145) notes that the South, the rural South in particular, is the "home country" for Northern blacks, and its ethos and symbols still have marked effects on the way of thought and behavior of blacks in the urban ghettos of the North. We may add that the influence of "down home" continues to shape Afro-American mass opinion, exercising a conservatizing influence on those living in the region but also, perhaps, on those born there but now living outside the South. This influence may continue for generations after migration from the region because blacks, unlike European ethnic immigrants, are linked to their "homelands" of Louisiana, Mississippi, Alabama, etc., not only by memories of a shared past but by physical contiguity and a common national citizenship.[17]

Chapter Five

Afro-American Culture and the Internal Dynamics of Mass Opinion

Our concern in this work is with racial differences in mass opinion and how these differences may be accounted for in terms of the competing explanations of class, interest, and culture. We are especially concerned to isolate opinion differences between the races that persist after controlling for the effects of social class. Such differences, we contend, may be understood as residues of a distinct Afro-American ethnic group culture. Yet, we begin cognizant of the fact that blacks in their attitudes and preferences probably share with whites what has been called "core American values" (Devine, 1972; Spindler, 1977). Even lower-class black Americans living under the extraordinary economic, social, and political constraints of the modern ghetto tend to exhibit, more so than not, mainstream attitudes, if not behavior.[1] As Hannerz writes, "Much of what any black American would do is the same as any American would do, while differences from the mainstream culture occur only in certain areas" (1969:15). This is why we choose to refer to the differences as "residues" that may constitute elements of a distinct race group culture existing within the larger context of a shared general American culture.

This is essentially what the results of our inquiry show. After controlling for the effects of class we find that black Americans are mostly like white Americans in civic attitudes and behavior and on attitudes regarding social or moral issues such as sexual practices, drug use, and traditional family values.[2] This is the case on some items even before the effects of class are considered, but once the large class differentials between the two racial collectives are factored out we find a considerable narrowing of the black-white gap in attitudes and behavior, pointing, as expected, to the powerful role of social class in homogenizing ethnic cultures in industrial societies. Even when apparent cultural differences are observed they tend not to be (pardon the expression) black or white, all or nothing; rather, they are shades of gray, more or less—a matter of quantity rather than quality. For example, it is not that blacks are religious, alienated, and liberal and whites are not; rather, it is that even after controlling for the effects of class blacks are—in a statistically significant way—more religious, cynical, and liberal than white Americans. This is all that is meant by the notion of an Afro-American cultural residue as we discern it in this study.

Having identified these three manifestations in mass opinion of Afro-American group culture, some effort, however tentative, must be made to explain how these differences are created and sustained (on this point, see Laitin, 1988:591). This is a difficult, necessarily tentative analytic project, given the nature of the data and methods we use (again, see Laitin, 1988, on how the mass survey inhibits this kind of analysis), requiring us to engage in historical and contextual inferences or speculation beyond the data itself. In addition to grappling with the historical and environmental sources of Afro-American cultural differences, any culture theory should, we believe, also explore the effects of these residues on other attitudes and behavior within the collectivity. These are the principal tasks before us in this chapter.

Sources of Afro-American
Cultural Residues

At the outset, statistical analysis of the data is helpful in identifying or, more precisely, eliminating and isolating one possible source of the differences—ethclass. The question to be answered is whether the observed residues are the effects of black participation and/or socialization in a working-class culture that is also characterized by these residues. For two of the three—religiosity and liberalism—no ethclass effects are observed. That is, lower-class respondents in the 1987 GSS are not consistently more religious or liberal than the middle class; therefore, the presence of these residues among Afro- Americans today may not be explained as an effect or carryover of participation or socialization or both in the lower-class culture of the United States. Rather, these attitudinal differences between blacks and whites are more likely manifestations of race group cultural differences to be explained on other than ethclass grounds. We turn to other explanatory grounds directly, but first the alienation residue may be interpreted statistically, at least in part, as an ethclass phenomenon.

Interpersonal alienation—a relative distrust or suspiciousness of the motives of others—is characteristic of lower-class persons in the survey and therefore, to the extent that blacks exhibit this residue it may be useful to interpret it as a carryover from their participation and/or socialization in a working-class community that is disproportionately large, and from which many middle-class, upwardly mobile blacks are a generation or less removed.

But the interpersonal alienation residue may also have its roots as a cultural phenomenon specific to blacks, arising out of the shared history and experience of racial oppression. One of the marks of this oppression is an exploitative, subordinate environment in which one's life chances are manipulable and often manipulated by others, black and white. (This is confirmed by a host of anthropological field studies in the Afro-American community, going back to DuBois' classic Philadelphia study in 1899. See also Dollard, 1937; Powdermaker, 1939; Drake and Cayton, 1945; Lewis, 1955; Hannerz, 1969; Rainwater, 1966.) This is certainly true historically insofar as whites are concerned, given the legacy of betrayal of the African in the United States from the signing of the Declaration of Independence down to the modern civil rights era. Thus, a relative suspiciousness of the motives of whites is part of the historical legacy of all blacks and probably continues to shape group attitudes. As Dr. King put it in his "I Have a Dream" oration, "America has given the Negro a bad check; it has come back marked 'insufficient funds'."

This theme is also central in the culture of Afro-Americans in terms of black-on-black as well as black-white interactions. The theme is found, for example, in black folklore with the character and symbol of the trickster (Dawson, 1967, Hampton, 1967), and the theme that the motives of others cannot be trusted is an abiding motif of the blues (see the classic studies by Jones, 1963; Keil, 1966; and more recently Palmer, 1981; see also Hannerz, 1969:150–56), as in bluesmaster B.B. King's 1970s piece titled "Nobody Loves Me But My Mother (And She Could Be Jivin' Too)."[3] And one hears it in everyday conversation among blacks, both elite and mass, as in the notion that "Blacks don't stick together" or "Niggers don't trust each other" as partial explanations for the persistence of the contemporary black predicament.[4] Indeed, in the relationship between black leadership and mass Holden identifies this cynicism as one of several "partially distinctive attributes of Afro-American culture" that diminishes the capacity of the community and its leadership for effective political action because of the routine activation of a "bitter cynicism and the almost paranoid fear of being sold out" (Holden, 1973:24).[5] The point here, then, is that although this cultural residue may be in part an ethclass effect, it also has deep historical roots in the experiences of blacks attempting to survive in an exploitative environment of racial subordination and betrayal of the "hope for deliverance."[6]

In chapter 2 we offered some thoughts, historical and speculative, on the sources of Afro-American religiosity. Nothing further can be added here; thus, we conclude this section by analyzing the sources of the liberal ideology among blacks.[7]

The etiology of liberalism as the consensus ideology among Afro-Americans has been traced in several recent papers (Hamilton, 1982; Willingham, 1981; Smith, 1984b; Jones, 1987). The consensus view elaborated in these papers is that Afro-American adherence to the liberal ideology is operational rather than philosophical, a question of pragmatic political interests rather than abstract theorizing. In one of his many contributions to the debate about the optimum ideology and strategy of black liberation—nationalism, integration, socialism, liberalism, etc.— DuBois frequently cautioned that "We face a condition not a theory" and that any ideology or program that gave promise of changing that condition should be embraced by blacks, whatever its sources, internal contradictions, or limitations. Historically, liberalism, the variant of American political thought that favors state intervention in the society and economy in order to promote social change, has been seen as more conducive to melioration of the black condition than the conservative alternative, and as a consequence liberalism has been embraced by virtually all strata of the black community since the antebellum period.

Ascendant black protest thought in the United States from slavery through freedom in the modern civil rights era holds that racism—the coerced subordination of black people to white people on the basis of the ideology of white supremacy—is the principal determinant of black life chances, and that intervention by the federal government is essential to secure black civil and political rights and social and economic justice. Thus, the operationally liberal character of black political thought, first because the conservative variant tends to look with favor on tradition and the status quo and is relatively hostile to social change, especially state initiated change. Second, conservatives tend not to favor government intervention in the society and economy, and when a role for government is recognized the preferred level of government is state or local rather than federal. Looked at this way, it would be virtually impossible for blacks, given their history and condition, to be other than liberal. Social change and reform is and always has been imperative if the subordinate status of blacks is to be altered, and federal government intervention in the affairs of the states and civil society has been critical throughout Afro-American history in improving the conditions of blacks.

Three historical periods of black advancement may be noted in liberalism's emergence in the Afro-American community. The first was the Civil War and Reconstruction era. The Emancipation Proclamation and the enactment of the Thirteenth, Fourteenth, and Fifteenth Amendments and the civil rights acts pursuant to them first rooted black thought in the liberal ideology. This is because it was an interventionist federal government that emancipated blacks and established constitutional principles and procedures designed to secure their citizenship rights against hostile state governments and private persons and groups. Also during this period the federal government established the Freedmen's Bureau (the first government social welfare agency), which sought to raise the social and economic status of the former slaves.

The second period followed the nadir of the betrayal of Reconstruction from the 1880s to the New Deal. Although Roosevelt's New Deal scrupulously avoided a frontal assault on the civil rights issue, its social welfare initiatives in employment, housing, cash assistance, and agricultural supports served further to anchor black opinion in the liberal ideology, precipitating a gradual shift in black voter support from the more conservative party of Lincoln toward the more liberal Democrats (see Kirby, 1980; Weiss, 1983).

In the final period of the 1960s, liberal Democratic administrations under John Kennedy and Lyndon Johnson secured passage of three major civil rights acts and launched the Great Society "War on Poverty."[8] The civil rights acts were quintessentially liberal in that they involved the intervention of the federal government in the Southern states to secure black civil and political rights, and in the economy and society generally to secure nondiscrimination in access to education, employment, and housing. The Great Society concept was also classically liberal, involving an array of spending programs that improved blacks' access to employment, housing, health, education, and legal services, and in general their capacity to participate more effectively in the political process. The War on Poverty is also associated with a significant reduction in the percentage of blacks living in poverty, and it had a dramatic impact on the growth and development of the black middle class.[9] This last period, especially, explains the extreme and homogeneous black liberal opinion profile, particularly on issues of the economy and social welfare spending. But again, in the context of black thought this philosophy is largely operational. As Jones (1987:25) writes:

> Understood in this fashion, one's position in the liberal-conservative conflict within contemporary liberal philosophy is not necessarily a predictor of one's position on the question of the optimum means for ending black oppression in the United States; however at least two factors make it appear to be so. The first is the central role which government, particularly the National government since the 1950s, has played in reducing racial discrimination. The second is the fact that the systemic debilities which account for much of the expansion of the welfare state, i.e. unemployment, inadequate health care, substandard education, etc., are more pronounced among blacks, and consequently amelioratory state action is often perceived simply as programs designed to uplift blacks, even though non-blacks may constitute a preponderant majority of the beneficiaries.[10]

The Impact of Afro-American Cultural Residues on Civic Culture and Ideology

We now look at the effects of the remaining cultural residues—religiosity and alienation—on civic attitudes and behavior in the Afro-American community. But first, the data on the relationship between the residues themselves are displayed in Table 5.1. No relationship is observed. Blacks of low, medium, or high religiosity scores exhibit the same level of relative suspiciousness of the motives of others, about 70 on our 100 point scale for each category. One might have thought that persons high in religious commitment might be more generous or charitable in their attitudes toward others, but these two cultural traits are unrelated in the Afro-American community (Pearson's R for the correlation between religiosity and alienation is .03, P = .286).

Table 5.1   Religiosity and Interpersonal Alienation Among Blacks

INTERPERSONAL ALIENATION (100 = HIGH ALIENATION)		
Religiosity		
low relig	72.9	p = ns
med relig	73.8	
high relig	70.9	

Guide to Tables in Chapter 5
P-values are reported for demographic differences if they are statistically significant (p < .05) or are of borderline significance (p > .10 < .05).

If a significant religiosity or interpersonal alienation effect disappears after controlling for another variable, a number is placed in superscript next to the name of the variable that is no longer significant. The number in superscript refers to which variable causes the demographic difference to disappear. A guide to these numbers is given below:

1. education
2. occupational prestige
3. income
4. subjective class
5. class mobility
6. sex

7. age
8. marital status
9. region
10. type of city
11. religion
12. religiosity

The Effects of Religiosity

Throughout history religion has been viewed as a conservative force in society, a mechanism of quiescence and control rather than activism and change. In Marx's famous phrase, religion is the "opium of the people...a universal source of consolation and justification...of the oppressed creature" (Marx and Engels, 1975:76). This certainly is the dominant view in the literature on the role of religion, the church, and the clergy in the struggle of the oppressed Afro-American in the United States. Myrdal, for example, concluded that in general the black church was a "conservative institution with its interests directed upon otherworldly matters and has largely ignored the practical problems of the Negro's fate in this world" (Myrdal, 1944:863; see also Dollard, 1937; Frazier, 1964; and Thompson, 1963, for similar generalizations about the role of the church in the struggle against caste-segregation). And in spite of the well-known role of the church as an organizational base in the modern civil rights movement (see Morris, 1984), studies during this period show that religiosity was inversely related to support for civil rights activism (Marx, 1967:94–105).[11]

The role of the church and religion in black politics is a controversial one, given the prominence of the preacher's role in leadership positions and "the ambivalent historical role of the church in Afro-American politics" (Reed, 1986:60). Yet, whatever one's view of black religiosity as a force for activism or passivity in black political life, it is clear that it is a major cultural strain in the Afro-American community that may have important effects on civic attitudes, behavior, and ideology.[12]

The Civic Culture

We look first in Table 5.2 at civic attitudes. In terms of political knowledge, efficacy, interest, and trust no religious effects are observed. Rather, respondents with low-, high-, and middle-range scores on religiosity exhibit roughly the same civic attitudes. In this regard, then, religion is an apolitical force, playing no role in structuring the attitudinal basis of the Afro-American civic culture.

In Table 5.3 we look at political behavior, beginning with organizational membership and participation. Here a religious effect is observed: The more religious respondents are more likely to be members of organizations, both political and non-political.[13] And they are much more active in organizations as participants and leaders. The religious effect here is clear and consistent: Religiosity acts as an inspiration to civic organization and participation.

The data on other forms of political activism—lobbying, community problem solving, and electoral activism (other than voting)—show no religious effects, but religiosity has a major effect on voting. Black respondents who score high on the religiosity index are about 20 points more likely to report voting in local and presidential elections than are respondents with lower scores (65 vs. 47 and 75 vs. 55, respectively).[14]

Thus, on the contemporary role of religion in black politics two things may confidently be said, insofar as the civic culture is concerned. First, religiosity does not have the "opiate" effects as suggested by the theoretical formulation of Karl Marx and the

Table 5.2   Religiosity and Civic Attitudes Among Blacks

POLITICAL KNOWLEDGE (100 = HIGH KNOWLEDGE)

Religiosity
low relig	36.9	p = ns
med relig	39.4	
high relig	43.3	

POLITICAL INTEREST (100 = LOW INTEREST)

low relig	47.4	p = ns
med relig	47.3	
high relig	45.0	

POLITICAL EFFICACY (100 = LOW EFFICACY)

low relig	47.5	p = ns
med relig	44.3	
high relig	46.8	

POLITICAL TRUST (100 = HIGH DISTRUST)

low relig	66.5	p = ns
med relig	64.4	
high relig	65.4	

Table 5.3   Religiosity, Organizational and Political Behavior Among Blacks

MEMBERSHIP IN ORGANIZATIONS (100 = HIGH MEMBERSHIP)

Religiosity
low relig	10.8	p = .004
med relig	14.1	
high relig	17.4	

MEMBERSHIP IN POLITICAL ORGANIZATIONS (100 = HIGH MEMBERSHIP)

low relig	10.7	p = .002
med relig	14.0	
high relig	19.2	

ACTIVE IN ORGANIZATIONS (100 = HIGH ACTIVITY)

low relig	9.9	p = .0007
med relig	13.4	
high relig	18.7	

LEADERSHIP IN ORGANIZATIONS (100 = HIGH PARTICIPATION)

low relig	18.6	p = .0000
med relig	22.9	
high relig	36.9	

Table 5.3   *(continued)*

LOBBYING (100 = HIGH LOBBYING)		
low relig	18.3	p = ns
med relig	22.5	
high relig	19.8	

PROBLEM SOLVING (100 = HIGH ACTIVITY)		
low relig	21.3	p = ns
med relig	20.6	
high relig	27.6	

ELECTORAL ACTIVISM (100 = HIGH PARTICIPATION)		
low relig	19.5	p = ns
med relig	20.3	
high relig	20.7	

VOTED IN 1984 PRESIDENTIAL ELECTION (100% = YES)		
low relig	53.5%	p = .0004
med relig	68.0	
high relig	74.8	

VOTE IN LOCAL ELECTIONS (100 = FREQUENT VOTING)		
low relig	47.4	p = .0001
med relig	56.0	
high relig	65.3	

empirical studies of Gary Marx. On civic attitudes and many forms of political participation such as lobbying, community work, or work in political campaigns, religiosity has no effect. But on organizational membership and participation and voting, where an effect is observed it is clear that religion, whatever its effects in the past, in the post civil rights era is not an apolitical force. Rather, it may be a stimulus to some forms of political activity.

Ideology

Religiosity has no effect on ideological self-identification (liberal or conservative) or on economic liberalism, as measured by support for spending on social welfare programs and government efforts to redistribute income or provide assistance to the sick and poor (see Table 5.4). There is a sense that commitment to Christian principles might incline one to favor aid to the poor and sick and other social welfare programs, as Martin Luther King, Jr.

urged and Cornell West (1982) postulates, but such is not observed here. Where religion does have an effect is on the social or moral issues and, as expected, its effect is a conservative one.

Table 5.4   Religiosity, Ideological Self-Identification, and Economic Policy Preferences Among Blacks

POLITICAL ATTITUDES—SELF ASSESSMENT (100 = CONSERVATIVE)		
Religiosity		
low relig	43.2	p = ns
med relig	44.2	
high relig	48.5	
SPENDING ON SOCIAL PROGRAMS (100 = SPEND LESS)		
low relig	19.1	p = ns
med relig	18.7	
high relig	21.9	
GOVERNMENT REDISTRIBUTE INCOME (100 = CONSERVATIVE)		
low relig	34.6	p = ns
med relig	30.6	
high relig	28.6	
GOVERNMENT HELP POOR/SICK (100 = CONSERVATIVE)		
low relig	27.4	p = ns
med relig	32.0	
high relig	28.4	

The data in Table 5.5 show that on abortion and the place of women in society, the more religious are more conservative, opposing abortion and favoring the more traditional role for women in family and politics.[15] In Table 5.6 data are displayed on attitudes toward homosexuality, premarital sex, and extramarital sex, showing the expected conservative effect of religiosity on these attitudes. Respondents with high religious commitment are more likely to view homosexuality and pre and extramarital sex as always wrong. Similarly, on the crime issues (see Table 5.7) there are no statistically significant religious effects with respect to fear of crime, but those with middle range scores are more likely to agree that the courts are too lenient in dealing with criminals[16] while those with the highest scores are more likely to oppose the death penalty. The highly religious are virtually unanimous in their opposition to the legalization of drugs. Finally, in Table 5.8 the highly religious are much more conservative on civil libertarian attitudinal predispositions, prayer in school, and attitudes toward communism.

Religiosity, however, did not impact upon voter choice in the 1984 presidential election. That is, the religiously rooted conservative strain in Afro-American society does not translate, as it does in white America, into a conservative vote.[17] In summary, the effect of the religious residue on Afro-American civic

Table 5.5   Religiosity, Abortion, and Women's Rights Among Blacks

ABORTION (100 = PRO-ABORTION)

Religiosity		
low relig	59.1	p = .0000
med relig	53.0	
high relig	41.0	

WOMEN TAKE CARE OF HOME NOT COUNTRY (% AGREE)

low relig	23.2	p = .0001
med relig	29.2	
high relig	46.3	

MARRIED WOMEN SHOULD NOT WORK (% AGREE)

low relig	23.2	p = .08%
med relig	28.6	
high relig	35.8	

Table 5.6   Religiosity and Attitudes Toward Sexual Freedoms Among Blacks

HOMOSEXUALITY IS ALWAYS WRONG (% AGREE)

Religiosity		
low relig	80.8%	p = .005
med relig	86.2	
high relig	92.9	

EXTRAMARITAL SEX IS ALWAYS WRONG (% AGREE)

low relig	60.6%	p = .0001
med relig	72.4	
high relig	81.7	

PREMARITAL SEX IS ALWAYS WRONG (% AGREE)

low relig	14.0%	p = .0000
med relig	23.7	
high relig	48.9	

Table 5.7   Religiosity and Attitudes Toward Crime and Its Punishment

FEAR OF CRIME (% FEARFUL TO WALK)

Religiosity
low relig	47.6%	p = ns
med relig	46.2	
high relig	51.2	

COURTS NOT HARSH ENOUGH (% AGREE)

low relig	75.2%	p = .06
med relig	84.4	
high relig	73.8	

FAVOR DEATH PENALTY (% FAVOR)

low relig	50.3%	p = .10
med relig	54.3	
high relig	42.2	

LEGALIZE MARIJUANA (% NOT LEGALIZE)

low relig	74.5%	p = .0000
med relig	79.9	
high relig	93.6	

Table 5.8   Religiosity, Civil Liberties, Foreign Policy Attitudes, and the 1984 Vote Among Blacks

DISAPPROVE SUPREME COURT'S DECISION ON SCHOOL PRAYER (% DISAPPROVE)

Religiosity
low relig	67.4%	p = .0003
med relig	80.0	
high relig	87.6	

CIVIL LIBERTIES (ALL QUESTIONS) (100 = ANTI-CIVIL LIBERTIES)

low relig	39.1	p = .0002
med relig	48.0	
high relig	51.0	

CIVIL LIBERTIES (EXCLUDING RACIST QUESTIONS) (100 = ANTI-CIVIL LIBERTIES)

low relig	37.7	p = .0001
med relig	46.6	
high relig	49.8	

SPENDING ON MILITARY AND SPACE (100 = SPEND LESS)

low relig	60.1	p = ns
med relig	64.2	
high relig	62.4	

Table 5.8   *(continued)*

COMMUNISM (100 = ANTICOMMUNIST)		
low relig	68.6	p = .05
med relig	73.8	
high relig	76.2	

VOTE FOR REAGAN (%)		
low relig	10.7%	p = ns
med relig	13.5	
high relig	11.5	

culture and ideology is to enhance organizational participation, voting, and the conservative strain in Afro-American ideology with respect to social and moral issues. Religiosity has little effect on civic attitudes and other forms of political participation (such as lobbying or work in political campaigns) or on economic issues, social welfare spending, and government income redistribution programs. Clearly, however, religiosity (except on the specifically moral issues) in the post-civil rights era does not have a conservative or narcotic effect in black politics. On the contrary, to the extent that it has an effect on political behavior, it encourages rather than depresses political participation.

The Effects of Interpersonal Alienation

Interpersonal alienation as a distinctive attribute of Afro-American culture has not been as widely investigated as the religious factor. However, we would guess that this cultural residue should have a negative effect on the civic culture, fostering nonparticipant attitudes and behavior. With respect to ideology, we would anticipate that high interpersonal alienation would have little effect, except perhaps on the social issues. This is essentially what the results show.

The Civic Culture

In Table 5.9 the data on the relationship of alienation and civic attitudes are displayed. Respondents with the highest scores are consistently and substantially less civic or participatory in attitudes, less efficacious, less interested in politics, and less trusting in political authority. The political trust relationship warrants further discussion. Theoretically, one would expect that persons who are distrustful of people in general would also distrust those in authority in the political system. But Aberbach and Walker, in their study using 1967 Detroit area survey data, found only a weak relationship between indicators of trust in people and political trust, leading them to conclude, "Clearly, political trust is more than a mere specific instance of trust in mankind. A strong relationship between political trust and trust in people would hold ominous implications for American race relations given the low level of trust in people which most studies have discovered among blacks" (1970a:1205). Yet, here we find a moderate relationship between the two indicators. Those high on the interpersonal alienation index score a low of 70 on the political trust scale, compared to only 58 for those low on the index (Pearson's R = .20, P = 000). In the absence of longitudinal data or studies we are unable to account for the difference between the two results. The concepts and indicators are similar, so this is not a likely explanation. The difference may be a function of different samples, but it also may be contextual—a phenomenon emergent in the post-civil rights era. Only further study can shed light on this important problem in the Afro-American political culture.

Table 5.9 Alienation and Civic Attitudes Among Blacks

POLITICAL KNOWLEDGE (100 = HIGH KNOWLEDGE)		
Interpersonal Alienation		
low alien	39.6	p = ns
med alien	43.2	
high alien	37.4	

POLITICAL INTEREST (100 = LOW INTEREST)2		
low alien	33.3	p = .005
med alien	44.7	
high alien	50.1	

POLITICAL EFFICACY (100 = LOW EFFICACY)		
low alien	33.4	p = .0001
med alien	47.8	
high alien	50.9	

POLITICAL TRUST (100 = HIGH DISTRUST)		
low alien	57.9	p = .0000
med alien	62.6	
high alien	70.1	

Somewhat surprisingly, there are not statistically significant relationships between alienation and most forms of organizational behavior (see Table 5.10). Only with active participation in organizations is the expected relationship observed, i.e., high alienation equals low organizational activism. If one generally distrusts others, one might be less inclined to join with them in organized endeavors (see Banfield, 1958, and Almond and Verba, 1965, on this proposition), but in general this relationship does not hold in the Afro-American community. The expected effects of alienation do hold for other forms of political participation—lobbying, community activism, electoral activism, and voting. As the results displayed in Table 5.10 show, those most alienated are least likely to engage in these salient forms of political participation.

Table 5.10   Alienation and Political Behavior Among Blacks

MEMBERSHIP IN ORGANIZATIONS (100 = HIGH MEMBERSHIP)

Interpersonal Alienation

low alien	15.5	p = ns
med alien	15.4	
high alien	12.5	

MEMBERSHIP IN POLITICAL ORGANIZATIONS (100 = HIGH MEMBERSHIP)

low alien	16.3	p = ns
med alien	16.4	
high alien	12.6	

ACTIVE IN ORGANIZATIONS (100 = HIGH ACTIVITY)

low alien	15.0	p = ns
med alien	15.8	
high alien	11.8	

LEADERSHIP IN ORGANIZATIONS (100 = HIGH PARTICIPATION)

low alien	43.2	p = .004
med alien	28.7	
high alien	21.4	

LOBBYING (100 = HIGH LOBBYING)

low alien	32.1	p = .001
med alien	23.8	
high alien	15.1	

Table 5.10   *(continued)*

PROBLEM SOLVING (100 = HIGH ACTIVITY)1		
low alien	29.8	p = .03
med alien	27.8	
high alien	19.8	

ELECTORAL ACTIVISM (100 = HIGH PARTICIPATION)1		
low alien	23.8	p = .05
med alien	22.7	
high alien	17.3	

VOTED IN 1984 PRESIDENTIAL ELECTION (% YES)		
Interpersonal Alienation		
low alien	72.7%	p = .02
med alien	70.6	
high alien	58.4	

VOTE IN LOCAL ELECTIONS (100 = FREQUENT VOTING)		
low alien	65.1	p = .006
med alien	59.8	
high alien	50.3	

Ideology

Of the 15 items dealing with the various dimensions of ideology—economic, social, and foreign policy—statistically significant relationships are observed on only five—military spending, the role of the courts in dealing with criminals, legalization of marijuana, homosexuality, and civil liberties.[18] Respondents with higher alienation scores tend to favor less military spending and harsher treatment of criminals by the courts, oppose the legalization of drugs, think homosexuality is always wrong, and are less tolerant of the civil liberties of deviant groups and ideas (see Table 5.11). In general, these relationships (except for defense spending) are as one might expect—the alienated in the black community tend to be conservative or traditional on issues of social or moral concerns involving sex, drugs, and deviant ideas and groups.

Table 5.11   Alienation and Ideology Among Blacks

POLITICAL ATTITUDES—SELF ASSESSMENT (100 = CONSERVATIVE)

Interpersonal Alienation
low alien	44.9	p = ns
med alien	45.3	
high alien	46.2	

SPENDING ON SOCIAL PROGRAMS (100 = SPEND LESS)

low alien	17.3	p = ns
med alien	21.8	
high alien	19.8	

GOVERNMENT REDISTRIBUTE INCOME (100 = CONSERVATIVE)

low alien	39.7	p = ns
med alien	32.1	
high alien	29.1	

GOVERNMENT HELP POOR/SICK (100 = CONSERVATIVE)

low alien	35.6	p = ns
med alien	28.2	
high alien	29.1	

ABORTION (100 = PRO-ABORTION)

low alien	51.3	p = ns
med alien	50.7	
high alien	50.3	

HOMOSEXUALITY IS ALWAYS WRONG (% WRONG)

low alien	67.5%	p = .002
med alien	88.7	
high alien	85.1	

EXTRA-MARITAL SEX IS ALWAYS WRONG (% WRONG)

low alien	71.8%	p = ns
med alien	71.6	
high alien	69.8	

FEAR OF CRIME (% FEAR TO WALK)

low alien	36.6%	p = ns
med alien	51.1	
high alien	48.0	

Table 5.11 *(continued)*

COURTS NOT HARSH ENOUGH (% AGREE)

Interpersonal Alienation
low alien	60.0%	p = .004
med alien	83.3	
high alien	76.3	

NOT LEGALIZE MARIJUANA (% AGREE)

low alien	82.9%	p = .02
med alien	88.0	
high alien	78.2	

FAVOR DEATH PENALTY (% FAVOR)

low alien	46.2%	p = ns
med alien	46.8	
high alien	50.9	

CIVIL LIBERTIES (ALL QUESTIONS) (100 = ANTI-CIVIL LIBERTIES)

low alien	39.7	p = .05
med alien	42.5	
high alien	47.9	

CIVIL LIBERTIES (EXCLUDING RACIST QUESTIONS) (100 = ANTI-CIVIL LIBERTIES)

low alien	38.3	p = .05
med alien	41.3	
high alien	46.5	

SPENDING ON MILITARY AND SPACE (100 = SPEND LESS)

low alien	53.8	p = .06
med alien	63.1	
high alien	62.2	

COMMUNISM (100 = ANTICOMMUNIST)

low alien	69.2	p = ns
med alien	70.4	
high alien	74.3	

VOTE IN 1984 FOR REAGAN (%)

low alien	10.7%	p = ns
med alien	14.4	
high alien	9.7	

In sum, this cultural residue affects the black political culture in three ways: It results in less participatory attitudes and more alienation from the political system, fewer ordinary forms of political participation such as lobbying and voting, and more conservative attitudes on some social or moral issues.

Conclusion

For historical, structural, and other reasons not perhaps entirely understood, the Afro-American community in the United States in the post-civil rights era is characterized by a relatively high degree of religiosity, cynicism, and economic liberalism. The religious strain in the culture has no effect on civic attitudes, but the alienation strain operates to foster a less civic Afro-American political culture in terms of attitudes. In terms of behavior, religiosity in general has the effect of enhancing certain forms of political participation (especially voting), whereas alienation has the opposite effect. Both residues have little effect on the economic dimension of ideology, but contribute to or reinforce a more conservative black opinion profile on the social and cultural issues. In the next and final chapter we look at how these residues and their effects on the civic culture and ideology provide a distinctive, almost "outsider" character to contemporary black politics and what this may portend for the future of blacks and American politics.

Chapter Six

Conclusion

In this final chapter we briefly review the findings in the context of the three theoretical perspectives, discuss the problem of class indicators and their relative explanatory power, review some of the methodological issues that may corrode some of the substantive results, and conclude with discussion of the implications of our findings in terms of Afro-American politics in the post civil rights era.

Theoretical Perspectives on Race Group Differences in Mass Opinion

Although each of the three alternatives for explaining racial differences in mass opinion—class, culture, and interest—exhibits some explanatory power, class, however operationalized, is clearly the most important. Most of the observed opinion differences between black and white Americans in civic attitudes and behavior and many of the attitudes with respect to ideology disappear after controls for social class are introduced. The consistent and predominant contribution of social class in accounting for racial differences in opinion in the post-civil rights era comes as no surprise, and once again reinforces one of the confirmed findings of postwar Western social science.

An ethclass effect is also apparent in some of the civic attitudes and behavior, as well as in the social issue dimension of ideology. Lower-class Americans tend to be less civic in many attitudes and behavior, less trusting of others, less politically efficacious, less knowledgeable and interested in politics, less participant in a wide range of political activities—organizations, voting, lobbying, and electoral activism—and more socially conservative. Black Americans, because of their disproportionate location in the lower class, therefore exhibit these attitudes more than whites, who tend to be disproportionately middle-class. This means that on some attitudes—political and interpersonal trust are the best examples—middle-class blacks, because of their socialization and/or participation in a lower-class culture, may retain these attitudes. It is difficult, of course, given the data and methods available to us in this work, to clearly separate out or disentangle the class and ethclass effects. The ethclass effect is clearest on the interpersonal alienation attitude, but the results there are not unambiguous. On some attitudes (economic liberalism, for example) where an ethclass effect may have been expected, none is observed, in that lower-class Americans are not consistently more liberal; therefore, the persistent strain of economic liberalism in black mass opinion is not just an artifact of black socialization or participation in an economically liberal lower-class community.

On the contrary, we interpret the dominance of liberal attitudes on issues of economic redistribution and government spending in terms of race-group interests. That is, black Americans, unlike whites, no matter their class location, see liberal programs and policies as a matter of strategic ethnic group interests. Like our interpretation of the data with respect to ethclass, analysis of black liberalism as an instance of ethnic group interest is an inference. The data and methods available to us do not permit the statistical demonstration of this relationship. But the inference is consistent with the historical development of black politics as discussed in chapter 5 and is consistent with the structural location of blacks in American society in the post-civil rights era.

In the civil rights era this class convergence in black interests was less apparent. Frazier, for example, in his polemic *Black Bourgeoisie* (1957) lamented the fact that the relatively small stratum of middle-class blacks failed to identify and provide leadership for the large lower-class stratum of black America. Banfield and Wilson (1963), in their study of urban black politics, also argued that the class structure of the black community inhibited the pursuit of race group interests in the city. Like Frazier, they saw the problem as emanating from two interrelated features of class structure: First, the existence of a large economically depressed lower class and a small, isolated, underem-

ployed middle class; second, the relative inability or unwilling-
ness of this middle class to identify with the lower class and
provide leadership for it. They write, "The relatively small
Negro middle class is separated from the lower class by differences of ethos and interests" (Banfield and Wilson, 1963:298).

In the post-civil rights era changes in both features of the
black class structure may have facilitated ideological convergence around race group interests. First, there was the growth
and development of a larger, more diversified, and occupational-
ly integrated middle class and a corresponding decrease in the
size of the lower class. Contrary to the class theory of ethnic
group differences, this very growth and diversification of the
black middle class may have resulted in class convergence rather
than cleavage on ideology. Hamilton (1976, and in Poinsett,
1973) argues that the black middle class that developed in America in the nineteenth and early twentieth centuries was largely a
private sector middle class, deriving its income from the market,
thus it could develop "class interests antagonistic to the black
lower class." In the post-civil rights era, Hamilton writes, "Basically the black middle class is salaried from the public sector and
this circumstance largely determines the sort of hard, self-interest
positions this class will take on public policy issues" (Quoted in
Poinsett, 1973:36). That is, since both the black middle and lower
classes draw heavily on the government, each has an objective
interest, apart from principled ideological considerations, in see-
ing the public sector expand—the middle class because of affir-
mative action and government employment opportunities, and
the lower class because of the expansion of government spending
on social programs. As a result there is in the post-civil rights era
a kind of "structural liberalism" that operates to bridge ethos and
status differences and create considerable ideological cohesion in
terms of the economic dimension of liberalism (on this point see
also Smith, 1978:21–22; Brown and Erie, 1981). Thus, we interpret black-white differences on the economic dimension of ideology as a matter of race group interest rather than as a specific
residue of Afro-American culture.[1]

This leaves two racial group differences that we interpret as
specifically cultural. Recall that at the outset we sought to identify three categories of American mass opinion: First, that cluster of attitudes where there are no observed racial or class differences, what we label generally shared or core American culture.
The second cluster of opinions is those defined in class terms,
where respondents, black or white, hold opinions in common

based on similar class location. Clearly, the great bulk of American mass opinion fits in one of these clusters. The overwhelming majority of Americans hold opinions that are current throughout the society or their particular class. This leaves the final cluster of opinion differences that we identify as cultural—racial group differences in opinion not explained by class. At least, this is the inference we make. Two such race group cultural residues are identified, religiosity and interpersonal alienation. Black Americans in a statistically significant way are more alienated and religious than whites, and these cultural residues, as shown in chapter 5, have important effects on aspects of the Afro-American civic culture and several dimensions of ideology.

Theoretically, then, each of the perspectives—class, ethclass, interest, and culture—are found to have some utility in explaining racial group differences in mass opinion. Class, as expected, makes the most powerful contribution to understanding of opinion differences, but it should not be employed at the expense of the alternatives. Rather, class in conjunction with ethclass, culture, and interest provides a more comprehensive understanding and explanation of contemporary mass opinion in the United States.

Before we conclude with discussion of the impact of Afro-American mass culture on the internal structuring of black politics in the post-civil rights era and on American politics generally, we need to return briefly to some methodological problems raised in chapter 1—problems dealing with operationalization of class and problems dealing with the survey as an instrument to study mass attitudes and culture.

Class and Class Mobility: The Problem of Measurement

The continuing debate, especially among sociologists, about the appropriate operationalization of social class—single vs. multiple indicators, objective vs. subjective criteria, education, occupation, or income or indices constituted by some combination of subjective and objective criteria in a single composite indicator—cannot be resolved here. Nor did we attempt to do so. Rather, we elected to employ both subjective and objective measures of the phenomena with multiple indicators of the latter. But what comes through very clearly in our analysis is that this approach is redundant. With few exceptions, in our analysis of scores of items dealing with civic attitudes and behavior and the various dimensions of ideology, the subjective measure of class and the three objective indicators operate in a consistent fashion, suggesting that each taps a substantively valid dimension of social class. This means, then, that to some extent whether one uses multiple or single indicators or, if a single indicator, education, occupation, or income is a matter of taste or a matter to be resolved on the basis of parsimony and the nature of the particular research problem one is working on. But what also comes through very clearly in our analysis (see Tables 3.2 and 3.3) is that by using education, occupational prestige, or income as indicators of class, the class differences among blacks are accentuated. All three of these indicators have 18 significant relationships (out of a possible 36) with the scales, compared to only five for subjective class and 11 for class mobility. Furthermore, the education and occupational prestige effects are usually independent of one another, while 12 of the 18 significant relationships between income and the scales disappear after controlling for either education or occupational prestige. Most of the income effects occur simply because people with higher levels of education or occupational prestige have higher levels of income, and not because income *per se* has an effect on attitudes or behavior. This is even more true for class mobility, where all but one of the 11 significant relationships between class mobility and the scales disappear after controlling for occupational prestige.

We are not saying that education and occupational prestige are better indicators of class. In regard to income there is relatively high measurement error, since many people either do not know their true income or are unwilling to divulge it. With regard to our indicator of class mobility, there is also relatively high measurement error because the status of occupations is likely to change over generations. In addition, the high correlation between occupational prestige and class mobility makes it methodologically difficult to separate out the effects.

We are also cognizant of the distinction between association and causation. Simply because one indicator is better than another indicator to differentiate among a number of indices does not imply that that indicator is better at measuring the underlying concept. Nevertheless, despite these caveats, the fact that education and occupational prestige are best able to differentiate among these 36 scales suggests the relative effects of these variables.[2]

Upward mobility—whether respondent's occupational prestige had increased vis-a-vis his or her father—was included on the hypothesis suggested by several students of black politics in the post-civil rights era that upwardly mobile blacks would hold attitudes and exhibit behavior distinct from the nonmobile. Conservative scholars such as Walter Williams and Thomas Sowell suggest that upwardly mobile blacks should be more conservative, whereas McAdoo (1981:162) found that upwardly mobile blacks were less religious. Yet we found hardly any differences among blacks using this measure; upwardly mobile blacks, for example, were not more conservative or less religious. These results may be a function of the crudeness of our measure and its possible contamination statistically with occupational prestige (using Kendall's Tau B there is a correlation of .75 between mobility and occupational prestige).[3] Nevertheless, to the extent that our measure of this phenomenon is valid, upward mobility has little apparent impact on attitudes and behavior inside black America.

Methodological Problems in the Study of Mass Culture

As indicated in our discussion of data and methods in chapter 1, there are inherent problems in using the sample survey as an instrument to study mass culture. These problems are compounded by use of a single survey involving attitudinal predispositions of a mass population at one point in time. Yet if one wishes to learn something of the culture of a population in the millions that is generalizable, then the typical ethno-graphic study will not do and there is no alternative to the sample survey. In a recent exchange with Wildavsky in the *American Political Science Review,* Laitin (1988:592) asks, "Can you do culture without doing ethnography?" Although he waffles a bit, basically he concludes that the answer is no; that in order to get at culture, properly understood, one must collect data "on the symbols, rituals and interactions that constitute and reconstitute cultures" (Laitin, 1988:592–93). While recognizing the limitations of survey data in "doing culture," we believe they have a place in cultural studies not at the expense of ethnography, but as complementary and/or supplementary elements. That is, one methodological approach should not be viewed as an absolute *sine qua non* of research on group or national cultures. Ethnographic studies offer valuable insights and knowledge of cultures, but they are limited in context and generalizability, and unless one is willing to forego learning of cultures at the mass level, there is really no alternative to the survey.

Further, in spite of the extensive (and useful) theoretical, methodological, and substantive criticisms raised about Almond and Verba's pathbreaking *The Civic Culture*, it nevertheless has yielded valuable and lasting insights into national cultures and, as Inglehart's recent article confirms, its approach and method allow us at the mass level to establish that at a minimum, "Different societies [may be] characterized by a specific syndrome of political culture" with respect to such things as life satisfaction and interpersonal and political trust (Inglehart, 1988:1203). In this work we believe that it is important to learn, as we have, that blacks and whites at the mass level in the United States today continue to exhibit different cultural syndromes or residues in such areas as interpersonal alienation, political trust, and religiosity, and that these group differences may have an impact on other civic attitudes and behavior. This much, we believe, our work contributes to understanding black and white political cultures in the United States.

A further problem here is the static character of the data and results using only the 1987 GSS. This means that we do not have the data to answer contextual or longitudinal questions. Cultural differences are the results of long, distinctive historical group or national experiences, and a single survey is obviously inadequate to sort out these historical effects and their impact on attitude formation and change over time. We must, as in chapter 5, go beyond the data to make inferences about the historical and contextual bases of observed Afro-American cultural residues. This limitation, however, characterizes ethnographic inquiries as well.

Any survey response is also influenced to a degree by the nature of the times in which the question is asked, by the salient events and personalities of the moment.[4] Political trust, especially, should fluctuate with political events and personalities since, as a number of scholars (most recently Abramson and Finifter, 1981) have shown, political trust is largely a measure of respondents' evaluations of incumbents. Thus, during the Reagan presidency overall levels of trust increased, albeit modestly, from 22 percent in 1980 who said they could trust the government most of the time to 38 percent in 1989, as Reagan left office (see Roberts, 1989). Similarly, after the battering that liberalism—the dreaded "l-word," in partisan Republican rhetoric—took in the 1988 presidential campaign, the *New York Times* (November 10,

1988) exit poll found the lowest percentage of self-identified liberals (18 percent) since it began doing exit polling.

Yet with the possible exception of political trust,[5] we would not expect the observed cultural differences between blacks and whites with respect to religiosity, interpersonal trust, and interest based ideology to be substantially altered by the context of the times. That is, these differences probably reflect enduring differences between the races (studies we have cited using surveys going back to the 1950s and 1960s show this for all three residues) that may vary somewhat statistically over time, but not enough to alter the fundamental pattern of group differences.

Our final methodological observation deals with the race differences paradigm in mass opinion studies. We have argued that the atheoretical comparison of black and white attitudes and behavior is an inappropriate research strategy because it tends to obscure rather than illuminate the internal dynamics of Afro-American opinion formation and, at its worst, treats the phenomenon as somehow deviant. Thus, an Afrocentric approach seems most suitable to the furtherance of knowledge here. That is, the black community should be treated as an independent entity in its own right because the race differences paradigm may be impotent in uncovering the internal factors that determine Afro-American opinion dynamics. The Afrocentric approach is increasingly being urged by senior scholars in Afro-American studies and used to good effect by younger ones (see most recently, for example, Woodard, 1988). We view this book as a small contribution to this trend toward Afrocentrism in studies of Afro-Americans.

Afro-American Culture and Politics in the Post Civil Rights Era: Whither The Future

On most items in the General Social Survey's 1987 inventory dealing with the civic culture and the various dimensions of ideology, black Americans resemble whites more so than not, especially when the effects of social class are removed. There is identifiable here a core of middle-class attitudes that characterize Americans of whatever race, predisposing them to a set of participant attitudes and behavior and a somewhat more tolerant set of attitudes toward deviant ideas, groups, and lifestyles. But there remain differences between blacks and whites not explainable by class, and these differences we infer to be cultural—a specific syndrome of attitudes that distinguish and set apart the races. In the post-civil rights era black Americans, even in the conservative period of the Reagan and Bush presidencies, remain a decidedly liberal group on issues of economic redistribution, government spending to meliorate social problems, and voting behavior. Blacks are also more religious than whites and are more cynical, suspicious, and distrustful of the motives of others, including those in political authority. We conclude our study with discussion of the possible effects of this syndrome of attitudes in black society and on American politics. That is, what are the probable political consequences for American society that its black citizens are relatively more religious, cynical, and liberal?

For a variety of reasons that we have touched on throughout this study, we do not see very much prospect for the emergence of a significant conservative political movement in black America. There is, as we have shown, a powerful conservative strain in Afro-American mass opinion that includes support for traditional family values, condemnation of pre- and extramarital sex, abortion, and homosexuality, as well as opposition to the legalization of drugs and support for school prayer. These attitudes are to some extent rooted in black religiosity, and they are especially pronounced among lower-class and rural Southern blacks. Yet conservative political leaders, black and white, have been unable to mobilize any significant mass support for conservative candidates on the basis of these issues. First, because white conservative leaders and candidates have tended simply to ignore the black vote, conceding it to the Democrats without a campaign—a campaign that might appeal to this conservative strain. Second, black conservative leaders (with the exception of such conservative clergymen as Los Angeles' E.V. Hill) have ignored the conservative social issue strain and its base in the lower class and the rural South in favor of appeals to the black middle class on the basis of their perceived objective class interests in lower taxes and less social welfare spending. The data and analysis here show that this is a tactical error since, to the extent there is a conservative base in the black community, it is to be found on social, not economic issues and among the lower class, not the middle class. Third, the data here suggest that even if conservative strategists were to correct this tactical mistake and focus on lower-class mobilization around the social issues, it is unlikely they would have more than modest success. This is because socially conservative blacks, unlike whites, tend to vote their economic interests instead of their social and moral concerns. This is seen most dramatically in the liberal voting behavior of highly religious, socially conservative black voters compared to their white counterparts, in the 1984 election. For the foreseeable future, then, conservatives are likely to remain isolated on the fringes of mainstream black politics.

Liberalism in the black community, we argue, is a function of race group interests. Black Americans, middle-class and lower-class, young and old, North and South, city and suburb, look around and see not Ronald Reagan's America of a shining city on a hill, but a city of despair, characterized in the post-civil rights era not by the dream of continuing social and economic progress but by the nightmare of a third or more of its citizens mired in increasing poverty and misery. All informed Americans are familiar with the doleful statistics and reports on the so called black underclass—the joblessness, homelessness, welfare dependency, children without fathers, schools that do not teach, crime and fear of crime, gang battles, and the multiple afflictions of drug abuse. Newspapers and television newscasts bring these statistics to life on a daily basis. But to black Americans this condition is not just a series of government reports or statistics, or an image on the front page or the evening news; rather, it is all in the family. Even relatively well-to-do middle-class blacks residing in the nation's well-kept suburbs know on a personal basis relatives, friends, or acquaintances afflicted by the multiple ills of the ghetto. And they believe the government could and should do something about these problems but instead has turned its back, leaving as one (white) scholar put it recently, "A Slavery Unwilling to Die" (Feagin, 1988). Thus, black Americans continue to hold liberal ideas and support liberal candidates and policies only to see those ideas, candidates, and policies overwhelmingly rejected by their white fellow citizens; even as in the 1988 election the very word itself was treated with derision, as profanity—the word that even the liberal candidate for president sought to avoid.

Thus, one consequence of this ideological syndrome in black society is the emergence and persistence in the post-civil rights era of a sharp race cleavage in partisan behavior. Not since Lyndon Johnson's landslide election in 1964 has a majority of both black and white Americans supported the same candidate for president. And the evidence is clear that a part of majority white disaffection from liberalism and the Democratic party is because of their embrace of blacks and their agenda on civil rights and the welfare state (Carmines and Stimson, 1980; Weissberg, 1986; Huckfeldt and Weitzel, 1989). This persistent failure in the post-civil rights era to be a part of the national governing majority, where one's policies and candidates are not only rejected but treated with ridicule, reinforces the historic outsider status of blacks in American society, especially among the well-educated, civic-minded, and politically active middle-class strata. During the 1988 election the *Washington Post* conducted a series of focus interviews with a group of largely well-to-do black Americans, finding a sense of cynicism, despair, and disgust about the campaign as it related to the status of blacks:

> These blacks describe a society increasingly tolerant of racism, a federal government insensitive to their community; a country with a diminished social conscience; and their communities wracked by drugs, cursed with poor schools and high unemployment. Their pessimism is a constant of every conversation and transcends class lines (Ifill and Balz, 1988).

This sense of despair and betrayal about the prospects for new, liberal government initiatives to address pressing social problems probably contributes to and surely reinforces the strain of interpersonal alienation in the black community. This cultural residue, as we suggested in chapter 5, may reflect current structural properties of the society, but also unique historical experiences of a group; in the case of blacks, a long history of betrayal and unfulfilled expectations. Thus, these two race group differences—interest-based liberalism and the culture residue of interpersonal alienation—may in the present period reinforce each other and serve further to distinguish and isolate Afro-Americans from their fellow citizens. William Raspberry, the black journalist, in a recent column titled "Another Word for 'Black' is 'Despair'," a piece dealing with a proposal by some elements of the black intelligentsia that black Americans now refer to themselves as "African Americans," writes, "After a quarter century of optimism regarding our eventual acceptance into the American mainstream, we sense a turning back of the racial clock in white impatience with black complaints of injustice, in the treatment of presidential candidate Jesse Jackson. That renewed sense of outsiderness may be the real force behind the drive to change the name by which we are called" (Raspberry, 1988).

This left-of-center ideological residue in Afro-American culture, when conjoined with a culture of high interpersonal alienation, may also constitute a force that could have serious impact on the American party system. Inglehart (1988:1214), among others, has posited that a culture of dissatisfaction and distrust may be related to an "extremist" vote or "extremist" parties of the left or right. In the post-civil rights era there has always been considerable elite and mass support for a black or multiracial third party of the left, and in the wake of the widespread mass and elite dissatisfaction with the way the Democratic Party treated Jackson in his campaigns for the nomination, it has probably increased in recent years.[6] A Jackson candidacy in 1992 that is again perceived by blacks as rejected by whites may congeal these forces, leading to a cleavage in black community presidential partisanship and a shift of some elite and mass support away from the Democrats to the Republicans or to a new third party formation.[7]

In his most recent book, Harold Cruse (1987) forcefully argues that black Americans should accept their persistent outsider status and build and nurture a "plural society," rather than continue to pursue the fantasy of an integrated America. In religion and to a lesser degree in education, the economy, and politics, Cruse contends that such a society already exists and needs only to be accepted and supported by the leadership. A principal vehicle to do this, in his view, is a black political party. The evidence from this study suggests that a cultural basis for such initiatives exist in post-civil rights era Afro-American society.

The most plural (separate and unintegrated) institution in Afro-American society is the church, based in the cultural residue of religiosity. Although the role of the church and the clergy is not as prominent in Afro-American politics as it perhaps was in the civil rights era, given the rise of a secular-based elected and appointed leadership (Henry, 1981; Smith, 1982:43–45, 80–81), this institution and its leadership, as evidenced in recent research (see Taylor, Thornton, and Chatters, 1988), remains the central sociopolitical institution in black society. This may be seen in its role as an organizational, spiritual, and fundraising base of the Jackson presidential campaigns and the continued disproportionate representation of preachers among black elected officeholders. The presence of religiosity as an Afro-American cultural residue suggests that the prominence of the church in Afro-American society and politics is not just a function of its extensive material resources and facilities, but indeed has a cultural base. Contrary to past theory and research, our findings here suggest that religiosity in the black community operates to enhance rather than depress important forms of political participation.[8] And, as we have argued throughout this book, religiosity, cynicism, and alienation have historically been interrelated. As Derrick Bell (1987:248) puts it in his recent book on the post-civil rights black struggle, "While the central motivating theme of black struggle is faith, the common thread in all civil rights strategies is eventual failure." There is, then, a kind of symmetry in the three cultural residues we have identified. Liberalism, cynicism, and religiosity congeal in post-civil rights era black society, and this combination could have radical implications for American politics in the second generation of post-civil rights black politics.

Scales and Question Wording

Religiosity [Alpha = .71][1]

About how often do you pray?

How often do you attend religious services?

[After identifying religion] Would you call yourself a strong____ or a not very strong____?

How close do you feel to God most of the time? Would you say extremely close, somewhat close, or not close at all?

Satisfaction [Alpha = .73]

For each of the areas of life I am going to name, tell me the number that shows how much satisfaction you get from that area: the city or place you live in; your nonworking activities—hobbies and so on; your family life; your friendships; your health and physical condition.

On the whole, how satisfied are you with the work you do— would you say you are very satisfied, moderately satisfied, a little dissatisfied, or very dissatisfied?

We are interested in how people are getting along financially these days. So far as you and your family are concerned, would you say that you are pretty well satisfied with you present financial situation, more or less satisfied, or not satisfied at all?

---

1. Cronbach's Alpha is a measure of reliability. It suggests how proper it is to create an additive scale. In this Appendix we report Alphas for all additive scales.

Taken all together, how would you say things are these days—would you say that you are very happy, pretty happy, or not too happy?

General Alienation [Alpha = .49]

[Agree or Disagree] In spite of what some people say, the lot (situation/condition) of the average man is getting worse, not better.

It's hardly fair to bring a child into the world with the way things look for the future.

Interpersonal Alienation [Alpha = .66]

Would you say that most of the time people try to be helpful, or that they are mostly looking out for themselves?

Generally speaking, would you say that most people can be trusted or that you can't be too careful in dealing with people?

Do you think that most people would try to take advantage of you if they got a chance, or would they try to be fair?

Knowledge of Politics [Alpha = .44]

We want to know how well-known the different governmental leaders are around here. Could you tell me the name of the governor of this state?

What about the Congressman from this district? Do you happen to know his name?

What is the name of the head of the local schools?

Political Interest

How interested are you in politics and national affairs? Are you very interested, somewhat interested, only slightly interested, or not at all interested?

Political Efficacy [Alpha = .55]

How much influence do you think people like you can have over local government decisions—a lot, a moderate amount, a little, or none at all?

If you had some complaint about a local government activity and took that complaint to a member of the local government council, would you expect him or her to pay a lot of attention to what you say, some attention, very little attention, or none at all?

Political Trust [Alpha = .42]

How much of the time do you think you can trust the government in Washington to do what is right—just about always, most of the time, only some of the time, or almost never?

How much of the time do you think you can trust the local government here in [name of local government unit] to do what is right—just about always, most of the time, only some of the time, or almost never?

[Agree or disagree] Most public officials (people in public office) are not really interested in the problems of the average man.

Organizational Membership

Here is a list of various organizations. Could you tell me whether or not you are a member of each type: fraternity groups; service clubs; veterans' groups; political clubs; labor unions; sports groups; youth groups; school service groups; hobby or garden clubs; school fraternities or sororities; nationality groups; farm organizations; literary, art, discussion, or study groups; professional or academic societies?

Membership in Political Organizations

[Of groups listed above] Do____to which you belong do anything to try to solve individual or community problems?

Activity in Organizations

[Of groups listed above] Have you ever done any active work for____? I mean been a leader, helped organize meetings, been an officer, or given time or money?

Leadership in Organizations

[Of groups listed above] Here is a list of things that members of organizations may participate in. Could you tell me whether or

not you have ever done any of these things as a member of___?
served on committees; served as an officer; given money in addition to regular dues; attended conferences or workshops; written
to newspapers or magazines for the organization; contacted government officials on behalf or the organization?

Lobbying [Alpha = .65]

Have you ever personally gone to see, or spoken to, or written to
some member of local government or some other person of influence in the community about some needs or problems?

What about some representatives or governmental officials outside of the local community—on the county, state, or national
level? Have you ever contacted or written to such a person on
some need or problem?

Problem Solving [Alpha = .57]

Have you ever worked with others in this community to try to
solve some community problems?

Have you ever taken part in forming a new group or a new organization to try to solve some community problems?

Electoral Activism [Alpha = .56]

During elections, do you ever try to show people why they
should vote for one of the parties or candidates? Do you do that
often, sometimes, rarely, or never?

Have you done (other) work for one of the parties or candidates
in most elections, some elections, only a few, or have you never
done such work?

In the past three or four years, have you attended any political
meetings or rallies?

In the past three or four years, have you contributed money to a
political party or candidate or to any other political cause?

Presidential Voting

In 1984, you remember that Mondale ran for president on the
Democratic ticket against Reagan for the Republicans. Do you
remember for sure whether or not you voted in that election?

Local Voting

What about local elections—do you always vote in those, do you sometimes miss one, or do you rarely vote, or do you never vote?

Ideological Self-Identification

We hear a lot of talk these days about liberals and conservatives. I'm going to show you a seven-point scale on which political views that people hold are arranged from extremely liberal—point 1—to extremely conservative—point 7. Where would you place yourself on this scale?

Spending on Social Programs [Alpha = .65]

We are faced with many problems in this country, none of which can be solved easily or inexpensively. I'm going to name some of these problems, and for each one I'd like you to tell me whether you think we're spending too much money on it, too little money, or about the right amount on: improving and protecting the nation's health; solving the problems of the big cities; dealing with drug addiction; improving the nation's education system; improving the conditions of blacks; welfare; parks and recreation.

Government Redistribute Income

Some people think that the government in Washington ought to reduce the income differences between the rich and poor, perhaps by raising the taxes of wealthy families or by giving income assistance to the poor. Others think that the government should not concern itself with reducing this income difference between rich and poor. Here is a card with a scale from 1 to 7. Think of a score of 1 as meaning that the government ought to reduce the income difference between rich and poor, and a score of 7 meaning that the government should not concern itself with reducing income differences. What score between 1 and 7 comes closest to the way you feel?

Government Help Sick and Poor [Alpha = .54]

Now look at this card. Some people think that the government in Washington is trying to do too many things that should be left to individuals and private organizations. Others disagree and think that the government should do even more to solve our country's problems. Still others have opinions somewhere in between. Where would you place yourself on this scale, or haven't you made up your mind on this? [5-point scale]

Now look at this card. In general some people think it is the responsibility of the government in Washington to see to it that people have help in paying for doctors and hospital bills. Others think that these matters are not the responsibility of the federal government and that people should take care of these things themselves. Where would you place yourself on this scale, or haven't you made up your mind on this? [5-point scale]

Premarital Sex

There's been a lot of discussion about the way morals and attitudes about sex are changing in this country. If a man and a woman have sex relations before marriage, do you think it is always wrong, almost always wrong, wrong only sometimes, or not wrong at all?

Homosexuality

What about sexual relations between two adults of the same sex—do you think it is always wrong, almost always wrong, wrong only sometimes, or not wrong at all?

Extramarital Sex

What is your opinion about a married person having sexual relations with someone other than the marriage partner—is it always wrong, almost always wrong, wrong only sometimes, or not wrong at all?

Prayer in School

The United States Supreme Court has ruled that no state or local government may require the reading of the Lord's Prayer or Bible verses in public schools. What are your views on this—do you approve or disapprove of the court ruling?

Abortion [Alpha = .89]

Please tell me whether or not *you* think it should be possible for a pregnant woman to obtain a *legal* abortion: if there is a strong chance of serious defect in the baby; if she is married and does not want any more children; if the woman's health is seriously endangered by the pregnancy; if the family has a very low income and cannot afford any more children; if she became pregnant as a result of rape; if she is not married and does not want to marry the man; if the woman wants it for any reason.

Women Take Care of Home

Do you agree or disagree with this statement? Women should take care of running their homes and leave running the country up to men.

Married Women Should Not Work

Do you approve or disapprove of a married woman earning money in business or industry if she has a husband capable of supporting her?

Fear of Crime

Is there any area right around here—that is, within a mile—where you would be afraid to walk alone at night?

Courts Too Lenient

In general, do you think the courts in this area deal too harshly or not harshly enough with criminals?

Marijuana

Do you think the use of marijuana should be made legal or not?

Death Penalty

Do you favor or oppose the death penalty for persons convicted of murder?

Civil Liberties [Alpha = .58]

There are always some people whose ideas are considered bad or dangerous by other people. [somebody who is against all churches and religions; a person who believes that blacks are genetically inferior; a man who admits he is a communist; a person who advocates doing away with elections and letting the military run the country; a man who admits he is a homosexual] For all 5 categories respondents were asked:

If such a person wanted to make a speech in your community, should he be allowed to speak, or not?

Should such a person be allowed to teach in a college or university, or not?

Suppose he wrote a book advocating_____. Somebody in your community suggests that the book be removed from the public library. Would you favor removing it or not?

Reagan v. Mondale 1984

[Asked if voted (see above)] Did you vote for Mondale or Reagan?

Notes

Preface

1. We explain the criteria for the selection of these dimensions of American mass culture in chapter 1.

Chapter 1. Theoretical Perspectives

1. Parts of this chapter are adapted from Smith (1988).

2. This theoretical eclecticism was found useful by Smith in a study of six New York City ethnic groups—WASPs, Jews, Irish, Blacks, Dominicans, Cubans, and Puerto Ricans. Smith (1988:183) writes, "On the basis of the data and analysis presented here, there is little to be gained by the continuing debate between advocates of class vs. culture vs. structural explanations of ethnic political behavior, especially if one perspective is presented at the expense of the other. Rather, each perspective may play an explanatory role. Structural considerations, however, explain well the tendency of the groups in this study to engage in ethnic political behavior."

3. A principal argument of critics of the civic culture relates to the attempt by Almond and Verba to link allegiant and participant attitudes and behavior to democratic governance and system stability. We agree that this theoretical linkage is problematic and it does not inform our use of it here; rather, we simply assume that citizens' attitudes about the political system and the extent of their political participation are an important dimension or component of mass political culture in the United States.

4. On the notion that these things should not be politically relevant, see Lasch, 1978.

5. We do not include such cultural preferences as religious rituals, taste in food, music, and dance, linguistic dialects or conventions, etc., because, although they are important in distinguishing ethnic group cultures in the United States, we believe they have little political consequence. Rather, they are, as Bell writes (1977:169), "nothing more than empty symbols," or in Patterson's (1977:57) words, "sentimental cultural patterns" with little vitality or relevance to a group's political life. In addition, even if we were to accept the hypothesis of the political relevance of these factors—such as, for example, the frequently advanced proposition that music is an important distinguishing feature of black and white political cultures (on the political relevance of music in the historical development and contemporary expression of black political culture, see most recently George, 1989, and Henry, 1990)—methodologically we could not deal with it given our reliance on the General Social Survey, which does not include items on tastes in music.

6. Reliability coefficients (Cronbach's Alpha) for these indices are reported in the Appendix.

7. Spending on space exploration is difficult to anchor in the liberalism-conservatism cleavage. Much exploration of space is directed at basic research. Yet many liberals (especially black liberals) have criticized the space budget, arguing that it takes money away from more immediate domestic needs and that it is structured primarily to support the military. Hence, we placed spending for space in the foreign policy and defense arena.

8. In the 1982 GSS but not the 1987, interviewers were asked to rate black respondents on a seven-point skin color scale from very dark to very light, permitting intraracial analysis of the class and attitudinal effects of color differences in Afro-American society. Substantial class effects were found, with blacks of lighter skin color more likely to possess higher education, family occupational prestige, and income. Lighter-skinned blacks were also more likely to be Catholic. However, no attitudinal differences were found after controlling for the effects of class (see Seltzer and Smith, 1991).

9. Education is a good single indicator for class because it represents not just years of schooling but also a whole set of life experiences in school, in the labor market, and in styles of living. It also has been found to be the most powerful single predictor of attitudes and behavior in cross-national research. Almond

and Verba (1980:21–22), for example, found that the educated in all five survey countries were more like each other in attitudes than they were like the uneducated respondents in their own countries. Educational attainment is also somewhat easier to standardize across cultures or nations than is occupational prestige or income.

Chapter 2. The Patterning of Racial Differences in Mass Culture

1. Among whites 62 percent are Protestant (16 percent Baptist, 11 percent Methodist), 27 percent Catholic, 3 percent other, and 7 percent with no religious identification.

2. We would have liked to test in a subsequent chapter the group consciousness effect on these variables as well as others, but the GSS does not include items that would allow us to construct a satisfactory indicator of black group consciousness. In addition, more recent work has called into question the basic relationship between race group consciousness and political participation. See, for example, Miller et al., 1981, and Tate, 1990.

3. The research problem with the concept of ideology (and the other basic social science concepts such as class, power, culture, etc.) is in concept formation, to be sure. But the major problem, given the absence of conceptual consensus, is that all too often scholars in the behavioral tradition, as we do in this work, allow the availability of and the properties of variables that permit ease of operationalization to dictate concept formation and indicator specification rather than the other way around, as it should be in normal science. For example, we agree with Mullins that ideology is probably best understood as "A logically coherent system of symbols which, within a more or less sophisticated conception of history, linking the cognitive and evaluative perception of one's social condition—especially its prospects for the future—to a program of collective action for the maintenance, alteration or transformation of society" (1972:510). Yet, with the data base we are working with in this study we are not able to operationalize Mullins' variables, especially the notion of more or less sophisticated historical conceptions linked to programs of action. Thus, we define and operationalize the concept in an admittedly prosaic way.

4. The apparent effectiveness of the pledge of allegiance and other "issues" related to the flag and patriotism used in the 1988 election by Vice President George Bush against Governor Michael Dukakis is a recent indicator of the importance of symbols in structuring mass attitudes and voter choice. Poll data reported during the 1988 campaign suggested that this "issue" helped to structure mass beliefs, especially among so called "Reagan Democrats" in the South and among southern and eastern European ethnic groups in the northeast and Midwest.

5. Of the three approaches, Lane's is the most capable methodologically of getting at Mullins' properties of historical consciousness and sophistication and their linkage to programs of political action. Lane's *Political Ideology* is quite instructive here on white, working-class historical understanding, more or less sophisticated, and its link to their preferences for political actions that maintain the status quo. Lane's basic findings on white working-class worldviews that predispose it to prefer political actions that maintain the social, economic, and racial status quo are confirmed by the recent work of Bostch (1981), who used a similar method to study working-class ideology more than a generation after Lane's work.

6. This approach is also consistent with the bulk of the current research on race and ideology (Welch and Combs, 1983; Welch and Foster, 1986; Dillingham, 1981; Gilliam, 1986; Hamilton, 1982), which facilitates comparability and cumulativeness.

7. In terms of percentages, using one illustrative example, although one-third of whites and one-quarter of blacks identify themselves as conservative, 64.4 percent of whites and 77.3 percent of blacks believe we are spending too little on education. Only 5.8 percent of whites and 2.5 percent of blacks believe we are spending too much on education.

8. Although it may not be strictly appropriate to compare these indices (the scales are not necessarily drawn in parallel), the results are still provocative, especially when seen within the context of the percentages discussed in note 7.

9. Although Nie, Verba, and Petrocik suggest that black opinion is also more liberal on foreign policy issues, this is more difficult to get a handle on because of measurement problems and because foreign policy attitudes tend to be more volatile and

event specific (e.g., attitudes toward wars—Korea, Vietnam—or specific countries and their behavior on the international scene—Israel, Iran, South Africa). For example, on attitudes toward defense spending as an indicator of liberalism-conservatism, opinion has shifted dramatically during the 1980s. For a discussion of problems in analyzing foreign policy attitudes along these lines, see Russett and DeLuca (1981).

Chapter 3. Class and the Patterning of Racial Differences in Mass Culture

1. In examining simple bivariate relations we use the chi square to determine statistical significance for nominal-level dependent variables, and we use ANOVA to determine statistical significance when the dependent variables can be treated as interval level.

2. Log-linear modeling is used to examine dichotomous dependent variables. ANOVA is used to examine the indices we created, which we treat as interval-level.

3. For the example of religion and education the largest difference is actually between those who did not graduate high school and respondents with some college.

4. We have only one index for representing religiosity. Therefore, the maximum number of significant relationships is one. For other sets of indices, the number of significant relationships can exceed one.

5. Our findings differ somewhat from Marx's when he examined racial differences in religiosity. Using data from a national survey, when he examined the various dimensions of religiosity, holding the effects of education and region constant, he found that blacks appeared more religious than whites only with respect to the subjective importance of religion. On church attendance Northern whites reported higher rates than blacks, while the rates in the South were about the same for both races. About the same percentages had no doubts about the existence of God, although blacks were more certain about the existence of the devil and whites were more likely to be certain about life after death (Marx, 1967:101). Marx's dimensions or indicators of religiosity, of course, differ from ours—they are more a measure of religious orthodoxy than religiosity. A recent study that sup-

ports our findings of the saliency of religion and the church in black life is Taylor, Thornton, and Chatters (1987).

6. Three-way significant relationships occur among general alienation, race, and four of the indicators of class.

7. For example, whites have a lower score than blacks for interpersonal alienation. For the education variable, among blacks it was those with the highest level of education who had the lowest score (most closely resembling the attitudes of whites).

8. Nelson (1979), in an investigation of "participant political culture" among New York City ethnic groups—Jews, blacks, Irish, Dominicans, and Puerto Ricans—presents findings that show holding class constant does not eliminate the independent effect of ethnicity on political attitudes and behavior. Rather, among whites, Hispanics, and blacks, ethnicity is shown to have a greater effect than SES on levels of political participation.

9. A three-way significant relationship occurs among trust in government, race, and class.

10. In fact, all three racial differences that occur based upon organizational membership disappear after controls for class are introduced (see Table 2.3). In addition, the average racial difference for the four scales (3.5) is miniscule compared to the majority of class differences.

11. In every instance where there are significant relationships between one of the class measures and one of the indicators of organizational participation, the attitudes of the highest class of blacks most strongly resemble the attitudes held by whites. In addition, in every one of these relationships the attitudes of the upper class of blacks is closer to the mean of whites than it is to the mean of blacks.

12. Occupational prestige appears to be the most influential class variable affecting political behavior, for many of the other class relationships disappear after controls for prestige are introduced.

13. Again, the average size of the class differences overshadows the race differences (see Table 3.2).

14. Among blacks, there are no significant differences between subjective classes. In addition, income is not significant

for three of the five indices of participation, and the two significant relationships connected to income disappear after controls
for education are introduced.

15. The three racial differences that exist on the abortion
and role of women questions disappear after controls for class
are introduced.

16. The average racial difference score (4.6) for these three
questions is clearly overshadowed by the class difference scores
among blacks (see Table 3.2).

17. This was vividly illustrated in the 1988 presidential
election as the Bush campaign effectively used advertisements
about a black convict who raped a white woman to portray the
opponent as a liberal on crime. As the political scientist Schneider observed during the campaign, "Crime, gun control, law and
order: The whole agenda originated in the racial polarization of
the late 1960s—black power, violence, the perceived failure of
the Great Society. And Bush uses the social issues to define
Dukakis as a liberal. The fear of crime originated in racial
fear...fear of crime is associated with blacks.... I don't argue
Bush is running strongly because he is a racist. He is not a racist.
But there is a racist component." Schneider is quoted in Lewis
(1988). The point he was making was first forcefully advanced
by Scammon and Wattenberg (1970).

18. The data for fear of crime are also placed in Table 3.8,
although fear of crime does not distinguish liberals from conservatives.

19. However, none of the three-way interactions between
race, crime, and class were statistically significant. This signifies
that the relationships between class and attitudes toward crime
are similar in the two communities.

20. However, the effect of education on attitudes toward
civil liberties was greater among whites than blacks—there is an
18.9 vs. 34.3 differential between those without a high school
education and college graduates. This differential was statistically significant.

21. We group attitudes toward school prayer with civil liberties. See Table 3.9.

22. Again, these items are limited measures of foreign policy
attitudes, although attitudes toward communism and defense

spending are undoubtedly important dimensions of elite and mass thinking in this policy arena, having structured much of the partisan debate, especially since the Vietnam era. However, we would like to have included questions dealing with more specific foreign policy problems, such as the Middle East, Central America, South Africa, and arms control. But, as we indicated, the GSS included only these two foreign policy related questions.

23. Welch and Foster elaborate this distinction between egocentric and sociotropic voting in their unpublished paper "The Impact of Economic Conditions on Voting and Policy Opinions Among Black Americans" (n.d.).

24. In any given recent year the FBI *Uniform Crime Reports: Crime In America,* issued annually, show that blacks are arrested for nearly half of all murders; about 90 percent of the victims are also black. And there is clear and convincing statistical evidence that the death penalty is imposed in a racially discriminatory manner. In *McClesky v. Kemp,* the Supreme Court was presented with statistical proof that race determines death sentencing in Georgia. Professor David Baldus and his colleagues analyzed more than 2000 murders in Georgia during the 1970s and showed, among other things, that a black was about 22 times likelier to be sentenced to die for killing a white than for killing a black. On hearing this evidence, Justice Lewis Powell, writing for the majority to uphold the Georgia statute, said the evidence indicated at best "a statistical discrepancy that correlates with race" and that "apparent disparities in sentencing are an inevitable part of criminal justice"; to rule in favor of the black defendant would mean that "We would soon be faced with similar claims as to other types of penalty." This argument prompted Justice Brennan to write in dissent that the Court's failure to confront the implications of Baldus' evidence manifested "a devaluation of the lives of black persons."

25. We were not able to isolate attitudes that might constitute elements of what we called "shared American culture." That is—strikingly—of the scores of items examined dealing with the dimensions of religiosity, alienation, the civic culture, and ideological issue stances in the economic, social, and foreign policy arenas, not a single one—not even attitudes toward communism or the legalization of drugs—is without a statistically significant race or class effect. Apparently, "core American culture" is at a very high level of abstraction, involving such things as attitudes

toward democracy, freedom, and equality, with relatively little content at the level of general social attitudes or political opinions (see Devine, 1972, and Spindler, 1977).

26. Assuming that Afro-American economic mobility will continue to occur. Class mobility was substantial for blacks in the 1950–70 period, but has slowed or completely stopped since then. It may even have deteriorated in the 1980s. (See Wilson, 1980 and 1987; Center for Budget Priorities, 1984).

Chapter 4. The Internal Foundations of Afro-American Mass Culture

1. The South, compared to other parts of the country, may have some intergroup theoretical power, since the South is historically more conservative or traditional and has exhibited a less participant civic culture, and blacks are disproportionately Southern in origins and current residence. Yet there is nothing in the theoretical or empirical literature that suggests that region plays anything like the role of class in explaining interracial opinion differences. Reed (1972, 1983) has found that white Southerners do exhibit a fairly high degree of region based ethnic group consciousness, just behind blacks and Jews in the United States (Hispanic groups and the native peoples were not included in his study). Yet for Southern blacks race group consciousness and identification clearly transcend regional consciousness and identification. Indeed, Reed and most other students of Southern culture exclude Southern blacks from their samples for this, among other reasons. Hurlbert (1989) also found that the South has continued to remain a distinctive cultural region.

2. Of the social science disciplines in the United States, Gordon and Rollock (1987:2) write:

> Traditionally, these sciences have been characterized by the examination of the relationship between social experience and the development and manifestations of individual, group, and systemic characteristics. A long tradition in these sciences is the incessant search for universal principles by which these relationships may be explained. Scientists working in this tradition look for principles or invest their notions with multi-cultural, multi-ethnic, nongender-

specific, and multi-contextual applications. Although there are some common denominators across all human experiences and groups, there is reason to believe that an overemphasis on the search for universals has been, at the very least, premature, if not mistaken. Indeed, in some cases, the search for universals has inhibited rather than enhanced the encirclement of social science knowledge. Despite the long history of this concern with the relationships between experience, behavior, and systems, insufficient attention has been given to the impact of unique cultural, ethnic, or gender experiences on the development of behavior and the social systems by which behavior is expressed. This neglect is probably the result of androcentric, cultrocentric, and ethnocentric chauvinism manifested in the Euro-American and male-dominated social sciences.

3. Marital status is not significantly related to satisfaction after controls for income are introduced.

4. The effect of region upon political knowledge and political trust disappears after controls for type of city are introduced, and the effect of region upon efficacy disappears after controls for education are introduced.

5. The relationship between sex and knowledge of politics disappears after controls are introduced for education.

6. The relationship between marital status and political knowledge disappears after controls are introduced for age.

7. The identification of young blacks with the Republican party (10 percent) is nowhere near the 40 percent that they obtained on the conservative identification scale. As for most Americans, especially blacks, the ideological label, as shown in the analysis of policy preferences, has almost no operational content.

8. The relationship between region and support for government spending disappears after controls for type of city are introduced.

9. The relationship between type of city and support for domestic government spending disappears after controls for region are introduced.

10. The relationship between region and support for government spending for the poor and sick disappears after controls for type of city are introduced.

11. Given that only 39 black respondents in the GSS lived in rural areas, caution must be used in interpreting these results.

12. The relationship between type of city and abortion disappears after controls for region are introduced.

13. The relationship between age and attitudes toward premarital sex disappears after controls for region or religiosity are introduced.

14. The relationship between marital status and attitudes toward premarital sex disappears after controls for region are introduced.

15. The relationship between type of city and attitudes toward premarital sex disappears after controls are introduced for either region or religion.

16. The relationship between type of city and attitudes toward the courts disappears after controls are introduced for region.

17. This is an important consideration in understanding Afro- American cultural continuity, since in 1974 the Census Bureau reported for the first time that the historic out-migration of Southern blacks to the cities of the North came to an end. In fact, in that year, for the first time in the history of the United States, slightly more blacks migrated from the North to the South, reversing the historic pattern (see U.S. Bureau of the Census, 1974:10).

Chapter 5. Afro-American Culture and the Internal Dynamics of Mass Culture

1. Hannerz (1969) contends that black ghetto culture is schizophrenic in character, given the disjuncture between attitudes and behavior. He argues that black Americans in the ghettos espouse mainstream attitudes and values in many areas of life (especially in terms of sexual relations, family life, work, and leisure), but the material conditions of the ghetto preclude their engaging in mainstream behavior. This point is elaborated by Hannerz in his final chapter, "Mainstream and Ghetto Culture."

2. This may lead one to wonder, then, what accounts for the vast differences between blacks and whites with regard to such

matters as the number of single-parent households, the percent of births out of wedlock, abortions, and drug abuse. It may be that these forms of behavior are concentrated in what is called the underclass, whose attitudes in the nature of things are difficult to sample in a general survey of the type employed here, or it may be, as suggested by Hannerz in note 1 above, that this discrepancy between attitudes and behavior is a function of people holding certain attitudes that their material circumstances preclude actualizing. Finally, as always in life and especially, perhaps, in sample surveys, people may say one thing and do another, either lying outright or simply saying what is thought to be socially acceptable.

3. B.B. King, the most popular of the postwar blues singers, has recorded scores of songs with this theme. Representative titles include "Don't Answer the Door," "Five Long Years," and more generally, "Why I Sing the Blues."

4. This latter suggestion is a generalization of Smith exclusively, although Seltzer has also noted the phenomenon during his experiences on the faculty at Howard and elsewhere.

5. For an interpretation of how this attribute, among others, affected the 1984 Jesse Jackson presidential campaign, see McCormick and Smith (1988) and the discussion in chapter 6.

6. This view of Afro-American culture is contrary to that of a number of scholars (Levine, 1978; Franklin, 1984; Henry, 1990, among others) who argue that despite the vicious, dehumanizing effects of slavery and race oppression, Afro-American culture developed what might be called a communalist ethos, an overarching sense of solidarity that facilitated blacks' working together. This "communalist" interpretation of Afro-American culture is substantially corrected in Rhett Jones' work in progress. Much of the communalist view is based on analysis of Afro-American folk material, but as Jones (1990:4) writes, "An examination of the folktales African-Americans told one another shows a shrewd, self-centered individualism among the slaves, not the cooperative communalism seen by so much of the scholarship of the 1970s. Not a single Brer Rabbit story celebrates communalism. The wily hare is the archtypical individualist, always ready to put one over on foes or, if need be, on friends." This notion also ignores the fact that most of the slave revolts, including the three major ones led by Gabriel Prosser, Denmark Vesey, and

Nat Turner were betrayed by other Africans, slave and free (see Aptheker, 1943; Kilson, 1964).

7. Analyzing sermons, spirituals, and folk beliefs, Henry's (1990) recent book forcefully restates the case for the centrality of religion in Afro-American culture and politics.

8. It is useful to recall here that Barry Goldwater, the 1964 Republican presidential nominee, and his then-protégé Ronald Reagan opposed the civil rights acts of the 1960s on conservative principles, i.e., that although racial segregation and discrimination were wrong, it was *equally* wrong for the federal government to intervene in the rights of the states and the liberties of white citizens to put an end to these practices. This further explains how conservatism came in the civil rights era to be identified with black subordination, and its alternative with racial justice and equal opportunity.

9. These generalizations about the effects of the civil rights acts and the Great Society to us are beyond debate, but of course in recent years there has been a debate about the efficacy of these 1960s reform programs and liberalism generally on black advancement. (See, for example, the conservative views of Murray, 1982; Williams, 1982. For the contrary view, see Ginzberg and Solow, 1974; Schwarz, 1988; Haberman, 1977.) For our purposes here, however, the debate is irrelevant, since whether the programs were effective is beside the point. Most blacks, elite and mass, perceive them to have been important in black advancement and this perception, whatever the reality, is what made liberalism the consensus black ideology in the post-civil rights era.

10. Theoretically, then, this racial difference in ideology is probably best accounted for by the interest theory rather than class or cultural theories. We elaborate this point in the next chapter.

11. Marx's findings on the inverse relationship between religiosity and political activism in the 1960s have been challenged on methodological grounds by Nelson and Nelson (1975) and Hunt and Hunt (1977). Their work suggests that, depending on the data used and how the variables *religiosity* and *political activism* are specified, religiosity's role in black politics is more complicated than Marx's study suggests, and that in Marx's terminology religion is best understood as both opiate and inspiration for political activism.

12. The controversy about the political role of the church has not abated in the post-civil rights era. Indeed, in some ways it has intensified. West (1982), for example, has forcefully argued that the evangelical religious tradition in black America is an important source for a liberation theology and strategy for social change, while Reed (1986) has rejoined that the black church and religion are "intrinsically antipolitical." Henry (1990:60–76) also sees the church and religion as a liberating, progressive force in black politics.

13. This tendency of religious respondents to join organizations is independent of religious organizations.

14. In fact, with the exception of age, religiosity is the variable with the greatest effect upon voting behavior.

15. Some of the religiosity effects upon these variables are striking. For example, 14 percent of respondents with low religiosity believed that premarital sex was always wrong, compared to 49 percent of those with high religiosity. With many of the other variables in this series the differences based on religiosity also exceeded 2:1 ratios.

16. This relationship is of borderline significance.

17. In the 1984 election white evangelical or fundamentalist Christians voted 78 percent in favor of Ronald Reagan, compared to only 11.5 percent of blacks with high religious scores and the associated conservative social views. On the 1984 white evangelical vote, see the *New York Times* (Nov. 10, 1988).

18. The four questions dealing with the role of women, sexual intimacy, and school prayer from the 1982 GSS are not analyzed here because the 1982 GSS does not include the same alienation questions asked in 1987.

Chapter 6. Conclusion

1. The question about the sources or explanations of the persistence of liberal-left opinion in the Afro-American community may end up like the debate about the persistence of liberalism among American Jews, especially middle-class Jews. Although there is substantial scholarly agreement about Jewish left-liberalism, there is little agreement as to why this is the case (see, for example, Cohen, 1980; Rothman and Lichler, 1982;

Fuchs, 1956; Lipset, 1984). Yet, like black liberalism, Jewish liberal preferences probably should not be interpreted as an ethnic cultural residue since, as Liebman (1979) points out, those Jews closest to Jewish culture, the primary carriers of traditional Jewish values—the Orthodox—have been and are today those most opposed to left-liberal policy preferences.

2. If one pursues economy of expression, as one almost always should, then single indicators are preferable to multiple ones. And, as we argued in chapter 1, of the three objective indicators, education is preferable to occupation or income in comparative ethnic or cross national studies in part because it is easier to standardize across disparate groups and nations, and partly because of previous work showing its powerful predictor role in cross national opinion studies.

3. McAdoo (1981:163–64) presents a more sophisticated measurement of mobility that includes four types or patterns: (1) Born working class, new mobile, (2) upwardly mobile in each generation, (3) upwardly mobile in parent's generation, and (4) middle class over three generations. The GSS black sample is too small to permit operationalization of these mobility patterns. Also, the Sowell and Williams hypothesis suggests that it is not mobility as such that should produce a more conservative ideology, but rather that the new post-civil rights era upwardly mobile black middle class should be more conservative. Age cohorts in the GSS are too small to permit adequate testing of this specific variant of the role of upward mobility on black mass opinion.

4. Yet another problem we should note in this context is whether reported attitudes of respondents in an hour-long interview are really attitudes or whether they are idiosyncratic responses that constitute "non-attitudes" resulting from a variety of errors in questionnaire design or implementation, sampling, response set, interviewer bias, race group differences in question interpretation, or simply the mood of respondents on the day, time, and place of the interview. Achen's (1975:1231) modeling of survey responses demonstrates that such errors may be substantial, but if the user of such data "has no idea of the size of these errors, as is often the case, [he or she] has little choice but to assume they are small and then proceed, treating the observed responses as direct measures of underlying attitudes."

5. Ever since the University of Michigan's Institute for Political Research began to measure political trust more than 25 years

ago, blacks have been found to be less trusting than whites, but especially since the 1968 election of Richard Nixon. Given the relationship between trust and incumbent evaluation, it is likely that the election of a president perceived to be sympathetic to black concerns would result in higher levels of political trust. For example, research at the local level has shown that having a black mayor greatly increases the level of political trust among blacks (see Howell and Fagan, 1988). Further, Bobo and Gilliam (1990) show that black control of the mayor's office in a city, in addition to increasing trust, also results in more efficacious and attentive participation in local political affairs by blacks.

6. In a national survey of black elected officials conducted in the early 1970s, 24 percent favored an independent black political party (Conyers and Wallace, 1976:31). In the 1984 National Black Election Survey 25 percent of blacks supported the idea of blacks forming their own party, and 53 percent said they would have voted for Jackson if he had run as a third-party candidate (see Tate et al., 1988: Tables 5.5 and 14.5).

7. Jackson has a chance to win (to get more delegates and votes than any other candidate) the Democratic nomination in 1992, given the experience he has gained and the rules changes he extracted from Dukakis at the Atlanta Convention. In a long, multicandidate contest Jackson might win 35–40 percent of the delegates, a plurality that would make him the presumptive nominee. The party then would face the dilemma of denying him the nomination, leading to black disaffection, or giving it to him, resulting in white conservative and liberal Jewish disaffection.

8. Also, contrary to most theory, high interpersonal alienation does not lead to substantially lower levels of organizational participation.

References

Aberbach, J. (1969). "Alienation and Political Behavior." *American Political Science Review* 63: 86–99.

Aberbach, J., and J. Walker. (1970a). "Political Trust and Racial Ideology." *American Political Science Review* 64: 1119–1219.

————. (1970b). "The Meaning of Black Power: A Comparison of White and Black Interpretations of a Political Slogan." *American Political Science Review* 64: 332–64.

Abramson, P. (1977). *The Political Socialization of Black Americans: Critical Evaluation of Research on Efficacy and Trust.* New York: Free Press.

Abramson, P., and A. Finifter. (1981). "On the Meaning of Political Trust: New Evidence from Items Introduced in 1978." *American Journal of Political Science* 25: 297–307.

Achen, C. (1975). "Mass Political Attitudes and the Survey Response." *American Political Science Review* 69: 1218–31.

Almond, G., and S. Verba. (1965). *The Civic Culture.* Boston: Little, Brown.

————. (1980). *The Civic Culture Revisited.* Boston: Little, Brown.

Aptheker, H. (1943). *American Negro Slave Revolts.* New York: Columbia University.

Babchuck, N., and R. Thompson. (1962). "Voluntary Associations of Negroes." *American Sociological Review* 27: 647–55.

Baltzell, E. (1964). *The Protestant Establisment: Aristocracy and Caste in America.* New York: Vintage Books.

Banfield, E. (1958). *The Moral Basis of a Backward Society.* Chicago: Free Press.

Banfield, E., and J. Wilson. (1963). *City Politics.* New York: Vintage.

———. (1964). "Public Regardiness as a Value Premise in Voting Behavior." *American Political Science Review* 58: 876–87.

———. (1971). "Political Ethos Revisited." *American Political Science Review* 65: 1048–62.

Banton, M. (1964). *Race Relations.* New York: Basic Books.

———. (1955). *The Colored Quarter.* London: Tavistock.

Barone, M. (1990). *Our Country: The Shaping of America From Roosevelt to Reagan.* New York: Free Press.

Bell, D. (1975). "Ethnicity and Social Change." In N. Glazer and D. Moynihan (eds.). *Ethnicity: Theory and Experience.* Cambridge, MA: Harvard.

Bell, D. (1987). *And We Are Not Saved: The Elusive Quest For Racial Justice.* New York: Basic Books.

Blauner, R. (1969). "Internal Colonialism and Ghetto Revolt." *Social Problems* 16: 393–408.

Bobo, L., and F. Gilliam. (1990). "Race, Sociopolitical Participation, and Black Empowerment." *American Political Science Review* 84: 450–62.

Bolce, L., and S. Gray. (1979). "Blacks, Whites, Race and Politics." *The Public Interest* 9: 61–75.

Bostch, R. (1981). *We Shall Not Overcome.* Chapel Hill, NC: University of North Carolina.

Brown, M., and S. Erie. (1981). "Blacks and the Legacy of the Great Society: The Economic and Political Impact of Federal Social Policy." *Public Policy* 3: 289–300.

Bullough, B. (1968). "Alienation in the Ghetto." *American Journal of Sociology* 72: 469–78.

Campbell, A., et al. (1960). *The American Voter.* New York: John Wiley.

Campbell, R., and R. Parker. (1983). "Substantive and Statistical Considerations in Interpretation of Multiple Measures of SES." *Social Forces* 62: 450–66.

Carmines, E., and J. Stimson. (1980). "The Racial Orientation of the American Electorate." In J. Pierce and J. Sullivan (eds.). *The Electorate Reconsidered.* Beverly Hills, CA: Sage.

Carson, C. (1981). *In Struggle: SNCC and the Black Awakening of the 1960s.* Cambridge, MA: Harvard.

Cavanagh, T. (1983). *Black Voter Participation: A Review of the Literature.* Washington, D.C.: Joint Center for Political Studies.

————. (1985). *Inside Black America.* Washington, D.C.: Joint Center for Political Studies.

Center for Budget Priorities. (1984). *Falling Behind: A Report on How Blacks Have Fared Under Reagan.* Washington, D.C.: Center for Budget Priorities.

Clemente, F., and W. Sauer. (1976). "Racial Differences in Life Satisfaction." *Journal of Black Studies* 7: 3–10.

Cohen, A. (1974). "The Lessons of Ethnicity." In Cohen (ed.). *Urban Ethnicity.* London: Tavistock, Methuen.

Cohen, P. (1980). *Jewish Radicals, Radical Jews.* London: Academic Press.

Converse, P. (1964). "The Nature of Belief Systems in Mass Publics." In D. Apter (ed.). *Ideology and Discontent.* New York: Free Press.

Conyers, J., and W. Wallace. (1976). *Black Elected Officals.* New York: Russell Sage.

Corbett, M. (1982). *Political Tolerance in America.* New York: Longman.

Cruse, H. (1987). *Plural But Equal.* New York: Morrow.

Dahl, R. (1961). *Who Governs.* New Haven, CT: Yale.

Darhendorf, R. (1959). *Class and Class Conflict in Industrial Scoiety.* Stanford, CA: Stanford University Press.

Davis, A. (1981). *Women, Race and Class.* New York: Random House.

Dawson, R. (1967). *American Negro Folklore.* New York: Fawcett.

Degler, C. (1977). *Place Over Time: The Continuity of Southern Distinctiveness.* Baton Rouge, LA: Louisiana State University Press.

Devine, D. (1972). *The Political Culture of the United States*. Boston: Little, Brown.

De Vos, G., and L. Romanucci-Ross. (1975). *Ethnic Identity: Cultural Continuities and Change*. Palo Alto, CA: Mayfield.

Dillingham, G. (1981). "The Emerging Black Middle Class: Class Consciousness or Race Consciousness." *Ethnic and Racial Studies* 4: 432–57.

Dollard, J. (1937). *Caste and Class in A Southern Town*. New Haven, CT: Yale.

Drake, S. C., and H. Cayton. (1945). *Black Metropolis*. New York: Harcourt Brace.

DuBois, W. E. (1899). *The Philadelphia Negro: A Social Study*. Philadelphia: University of Pennsylvania.

Elliot, J. (1986). *Black Voices in American Politics*. New York: Harcourt Brace Jovanovich.

Engstrom, R. (1970). "Race and Compliance: Differential Political Socialization." *Polity* 3: 100–11.

Eisinger, P. (1982). "Black Employment in Municipal Jobs." *American Political Science Review* 76: 380–92.

Esslinger, D. (1974). *Immigrants and the City in a Nineteenth Century City*. Port Washington, NY: Kennikat.

Fanon, F. (19567). *Black Skin, White Mask*. New York: Grove.

Farley, R. (1970). "The Changing Distribution of Negroes Within Metropolitan Areas: The Emergence of Black Suburbs." *American Journal of Sociology*. 75: 524–35.

Farley, R., and W. Allen. (1986). *The Color Line and the Quality of Life in America*. New York: Russell Sage.

Feagin, J. (1988). "A Slavery Unwilling to Die." *Journal of Black Studies* 18: 451–69.

Finifter, A. (1970). "Dimensions of Alienation." *American Political Science Review* 64: 389–410.

Franklin, V. P. (1984). *Black Self-Determination*. Westport, CT: Lawrence Hill.

Frazier, E. (1949). *The Negro in the United States*. New York: Macmillan.

————. (1957). *Black Bourgeoisie*. Glencoe, IL: Free Press.

————. (1962). *The Negro Church*. New York: Schocken.

Fredrickson, G. (1971). *The Black Image in the White Mind*. New York: Harper & Row.

Free, L., and H. Cantril. (1968). *The Political Beliefs of Americans*. New York: Simon & Schuster.

Fromm, E. (1967). *Marx's Concept of Man*. New York: Ungar.

Fuchs, L. (1956). *The Political Behavior of American Jews*. Glencoe, IL: Free Press.

Gambino, R. (1974). *Blood of My Blood: The Dilemma of the Italian-Americans*. New York: Doubleday.

Gans, H. (1962). *Urban Villagers: Class and Group Life in an Italian-American Community*. New York: Free Press.

————. (1967). *The Levittowners: Ways of Life and Politics in a New Suburban Community*. New York: Vintage Books.

George, N. (1989). *The Death of Rhythm and Blues*. New York: Pantheon.

Gilliam, F. (1986). "Black America: Divided by Class." *Public Opinion* 12: 53–57.

Gilliam, F., and K. Whitby. (1989). "Race, Class, and Attitudes toward Social Welfare Spending: An Ethclass Interpretation" *Social Science Quarterly* 70:89–100.

Ginzberg, E., and R. Solow. (1974). "The Great Society: Lessons for the Future." Special Issue, *The Public Interest*, 5.

Glazer, N., and D. Moynihan. (1963). *Beyond the Melting Pot*. Cambridge, MA: MIT.

Glenn, N., and E. Gotard. (1977). "Religion Among Blacks in the United States: Some Recent Trends and Current Characteristics." *American Journal of Sociology* 83: 443–51.

Goering, J. (1971). "The Emergence of Ethnic Interests: A Case of Serendipity." *Social Forces* 49: 379–84.

Gordon, E., and D. Rollock. (1987). "Commincentric Frames of Reference in Pursuit of Knowledge." Unpublished manuscript, Program in Afro-American Studies, Yale University.

Gordon, M. (1964). *Assimilation in America: The Role of Race, Religion and National Origin.* New York: Oxford.

————. (1975). "Toward a General Theory of Racial and Ethnic Group Relations." In N. Glazer and D. Moynihan. (eds.). *Ethnicity: Theory and Experience.* Cambridge, MA: Harvard.

Greeley, A. (1974). *Ethnicity in the United States.* New York: John Wiley.

Guterbock, T., and B. London. (1983). "Race, Political Orientation and Participation: A Test of Four Competing Theories." *American Sociological Review* 48: 191–206.

Haberman, R. (1977). *A Decade of Anti-Poverty Programs.* New York: Academic Press.

Hamilton, C. (1976). "Public Policy and Some Political Consequences." In M. Barnett and J. Hefner. (eds.). *Public Policy for the Black Community.* New York: Alfred.

————. (1982). "Measuring Black Conservatism." In *The State of Black America.* New York: National Urban League.

Hagner, P., and John Pierce. (1984). "Racial Differences and Political Conceptualization" *Western Political Quarterly* 37:212–35.

Hampton, B. (1967). "On Identification and Negro Tricksters." *Southern Folklore Quarterly* 31: 55–65.

Hannerz, U. (1969). *Soulside: Studies in Ghetto Culture and Community.* New York: Columbia.

Harding, V. (1981). *There is a River: A History of the Afro-American Freedom Struggle.* New York: Basic Books.

Hawkins, B., and R. Lorinkas. (1970). *The Ethnic Factor in American Politics.* Columbus, OH: Merrill.

Hechter, M. (1978). "Group Formation and the Cultural Division of Labor." *American Journal of Sociology* 84: 293–318.

————. (1975). *Internal Colonialism: The Celtic Fringe in British National Development.* Berkeley, CA: University of California.

Hennessy, T. (1970). "Problems in Concept Formation: Ethos Theory and the Comparative Study of Urban Politics." *Midwest Journal of Political Science* 24: 537–64.

Henry, C. (1981). "*Ebony*'s Elite: America's Most Influential Blacks." *Phylon* 42: 120–32.

————. (1990). *Culture and African-American Politics.* Bloomington, IN: Indiana University Press.

Hershberg, T., et al. (1979). "A Tale of Three Cities: Blacks and Immigrants in Philadelphia, 1850–1880, and 1970." *The Annals* 441: 55–81.

Herskovits, M. (1941). *The Myth of the Negro Past.* New York: Harper.

Herson, L. (1975). "Tolerance, Consensus, and the Democratic Creed: A Contextual Explanation" *Journal of Politics* 37:1007–32.

Higham, J. (1955). *Strangers in the Land: Patterns of American Nativism.* New Brunswick, NJ: Rutgers.

Holden, M. (1973). *The Politics of the Black "Nation".* New York: Chandler.

Howell, S., and D. Fagan. (1988). "Race and Trust: Testing the Political Reality Model" *Public Opinion Quarterly* 52: 343–50.

Howitt, A., and R. Moniz. (1976). "Ethnic Identity, Political Organization and Political Structure." Paper presented at the Annual Meeting of the American Political Science Association, Chicago.

Huckfeldt, R., and C. Weitzel. (1989). *Race and the Decline of Class in American Politics.* Urbana, IL: University of Illinois Press.

Huggins, N. (1971). "Afro-American History: Myths, Heroes and Reality." In M. Kilson, D. Fox, and N. Huggins. (eds.). *Key Issues in the Afro-American Experience.* New York: Harcourt Brace.

Hunt, L., and J. Hunt. (1977). "Black Religion as Both Opiate and Inspiration of Civil Rights Militancy: Putting Marx's Data to the Tests." *Social Forces* 55: 1–14.

Hurlbert, J. S. (1989). "The Southern Region: A Test of the Hypothesis of Cultural Distinctiveness." *The Sociological Quarterly* 30: 245–266.

Ifill, G., and D. Balz. (1988). "We Want a Piece of the Pie: Middle Class Blacks are Downbeat About the Campaign." *Washington Post National Weekly Edition*, October 3–9, pp. 6–7.

Inglehart, R. (1988). "The Renaissance of Political Culture." *American Political Science Review* 82: 1203–30.

Institute for Contemporary Studies. (1981). *The Fairmount Papers*. San Francisco, CA: Institute for Contemporary Studies.

Isajiw, W. (1974). "Definitions of Ethnicity." *Ethnicity* 1: 111–24.

Jackman, M., and R. Jackman. (1983). *Class Awareness in the United States*. Berkeley, CA: University of California.

Jackson, K. (1972). "Metropolitan Government vs. Suburban Autonomy: Politics on the Crabgrass Frontier." In K. Jackson and S. Schultz. (eds.). *Cities in American History*. New York: Knopf.

Jahn, J. (1961). *Muntu*. New York: Grove.

Jones, L. (1963). *Blues People*. New York: Morrow.

Jones, M. (1972). "A Frame of Reference for Black Politics." In L. Henderson (ed.). *Black Political Life in the United States*. New York: Chandler.

————. (1986). Personal communications.

————. (1987). "The Political Thought of Black Conservatives: An Analysis, Explanation and Interpretation." In F. Jones and M. Adams. (eds.). *Readings in American Politics*. Dubuque, IA: Kendall/Hunt.

Jones, R. (1990). "The Myth of Afro-American Communalism: Elements of a Black Political Psychology." Unpublished manuscript, Brown University.

Jordan, W. (1968). *White Over Black*. Chapel Hill, NC: University of North Carolina.

Katznelson, I. (1972). "Comparative Studies of Race and Ethnicity: Plural Analysis and Beyond." *Comparative Politics*. 1: 135–54.

————. (1981). *City Trenches: Urban Politics and the Patterning of Class in the United States*. Chicago: University of Chicago Press.

Keil, C. (1966). *Urban Blues*. Chicago: University of Chicago.

Killan, L., and J. Griggs. (1962). "Urbanism, Race and Anomie." *American Journal of Sociology* 67: 661–65.

Kilson, M. (1964). "Toward Freedom: An Analysis of Slave Revolts in the United States." *Phylon* 25: 175–87.

Kirby, J. (1980). *Black Americans and the Roosevelt Era.* Knoxville, TN: University of Tennessee.

Krickus, R. (1976). *Pursuing the American Dream: White Ethnics and the New Populism.* New York: Anchor.

Kroeber, A., and C. Kluckhohn. (1952). *Culture: A Critical Review of Concepts and Definitions.* New York: Peabody Museum of Archaeology and Ethnology. 47 #1.

Laitin, D. (1988). "Political Culture and Political Preferences." *American Political Science Review* 82: 590–93.

Landry, B. (1987). *The New Black Middle Class.* Berkeley, CA: University of California.

Lane, R. (1962). *Political Ideology.* New York: Free Press.

Lasch, C. (1978). *The Culture of Narcissism.* New York: Norton.

Lehman, N. (1986). "The Origins of the Underclass." *The Atlantic Monthly.* June, 1986, July, 1986, pp. 31–55, 54–86.

Lenski, G. (1976). *The Religious Factor: A Sociological Study of Religion's Impact on Politics, Economics and Family.* Garden City, NJ: Doubleday.

Levine, L. (1977). *Black Culture and Black Consciousness: Afro-American Folk Thought From Slavery to Freedom.* New York: Oxford.

Lewis, A. (1988). "The Dirty Little Secret." *New York Times.* October 20, 1988, p. 23.

Lewis, D. (1977). "A Repose to Inequality: Black Women, Racism and Sexism." *Signs* 3: 339–61.

Lewis, H. (1955). *Blackways of Kent.* Chapel Hill, NC: University of North Carolina.

Liebman, A. (1979). *Jews and the Left.* New York: John Wiley.

Lijphart, A. (1980). "The Structure of Inference." In G. Almond and S. Verba. (eds.). *The Civic Culture Revisited.* Boston: Little, Brown.

Lipset, S. (1984). "Jews Are Still Liberal and Proud of It." *Washington Post*, December 30, p. C1.

Lipset, S., and W. Schneider. (1987). *The Confidence Gap*. Baltimore, MD: Johns Hopkins.

London, B. (1975). "Racial Differences in Social and Political Participation: It's Not Simply a Matter of Black and White." *Social Science Quarterly* 56: 274–86.

London, B., and M. Giles. (1987). "Black Participation: Compensation or Ethnic Identification." *Journal of Black Studies* 18: 20–44.

Loury, G. (1985). "The Moral Quandary of the Black Community." *The Public Interest* 15: 11–17.

Luttbeg, N., and M. Martinez. (1987). "Demographic Differences in Opinion, 1956–84." Unpublished manuscript, Department of Political Science, Texas A & M University.

McAdoo, H. (1981). "Patterns of Upward Mobility in Black Families." In McAdoo (ed.). *Black Families*. Beverly Hills, CA: Sage.

McCormick, J., A. Thornton, and W. Hill. (1988). "Partisan Preferences and Attitudes Toward a 1988 Jackson Presidential Bid: Views of the Post-Civil Rights Generation." Unpublished manuscript, Department of Political Science, Howard University.

McCormick, J., and R. Smith. (1988). "Through the Prism of Afro-American Culture: An Interpretation of the Jackson Campaign Style." In L. Barker and R. Walters. (eds.). *Jesse Jackson's Presidential Campaign: Challenge and Change in American Politics*. Urbana, IL: University of Illinois.

McLemore, L. (1972). "Toward a Theory of Black Politics: The Black and Ethnic Models Revisited." *Journal of Black Studies* 1: 323–31.

McPherson, J. (1977). "Correlates of Social Participation: A Comparison of Ethnic Community and Compensatory Theories." *Social Science Quarterly* 18: 197–208.

Malveaux, J. (1987). "Current Economic Trends and Black Feminist Consciousness." *The Black Scholar* 16: 28–39.

Marx, G. (1967). *Protest and Prejudice: A Study of Belief in Black America*. New York: Harper.

Marx, K., and F. Engels. (1975). *Collected Works.* New York: International.

Marvick, D. (1965). "The Political Socialization of the American Negro." *The Annals* 361: 112–27.

Merton, R. (1949). "Social Structure and Anomie." In Merton, *Social Theory and Social Structure.* Glencoe, IL: Free Press.

Meszaros, I. (1970). *Marx's Theory of Alienation.* London: Merlin Press.

Meyers, G. (1943). *A History of Bigotry in the United States.* New York: Random House.

Middleton, R. (1963). "Alienation, Race and Education." *American Sociological Review* 28: 793–97.

Milbrath, L. (1965). *Political Participation.* Chicago: Rand McNally.

Miller, A., et al. (1981). "Group Consciousness and Political Participation." *American Journal of Political Science* 25: 495–511.

Mindel, C., and R. Habenstein. (eds.). (1976). *Ethnic Families in America.* New York: Elisvier.

Mitchell, A., T. Brown, and A. Raine. (1973). "Social Conflict and Political Estrangement, 1958–72." Paper prepared for presentation at the Annual Meeting of the Midwest Political Science Association, Chicago.

Mock, J. (1982). "The Black Vote Output: Black Political Executives, 1961–80." Paper prepared for presentation at the Annual Meeting of the Midwest Political Science Association, Milwaukee.

Morris, A. (1984). *The Origins of the Civil Rights Movement.* New York: Basic.

Morris, M. (1975). *The Politics of Black America.* New York: Harpers.

Mullins, W. (1972). "On the Concept of Ideology in Political Science." *American Political Science Review* 66: 489–509.

Murray, C. (1982). *Losing Ground.* New York: Basic Books.

Myrdal, G. (1944; 1967). *An American Dilemma.* 2 Vols. New York: Harpers.

Natchez, P. (1985). *Images of Voting/Visions of Democracy.* New York: Basic Books.

National Conference of Christians and Jews. (1978). *A Study of Attitudes Toward Racial and Religious Minorities and Toward Women.* New York: Louis Harris Associates.

Nelson, D. (1979). "Ethnicity and Socioeconomic Status as Sources of Participation: The Case for Ethnic Political Culture." *American Political Science Review* 73: 1024–38.

Nelson, H., and A. Nelson. (1975). *The Black Church in the Sixties.* Lexington: University of Kentucky Press.

New York Times. "Portrait of the Electorate." November 10, 1988.

Nie, N., and K. Anderson. (1974). "Mass Beliefs Revisited: Political Change and Attitude Structure." *Journal of Politics* 36: 541–91.

Nie, N., S. Verba, and J. Petrocik. (1976). *The Changing American Voter.* Cambridge, MA: Harvard.

Novak, M. (1971). *The Rise of the Unmeltable Ethnics: Politics and Culture in the Seventies.* New York: Macmillan.

Nunn, C., H. Crockett, and J. Williams. (1978). *Tolerance for Non-Conformity.* San Francisco: Jossey-Bass.

Ollman, B. (1970). *Marx's Conception of Man in Capitalist Societies.* New York: Free Press.

Olsen, M. (1969). "Social and Political Participation of Blacks." *American Sociological Review* 35: 609–96.

Palmer, R. (1981). *Deep Blues.* New York: Viking.

Parant, W., and P. Stekler. (1985). "The Political Implications of Stratification in the Black Community." *Western Political Quarterly* 38: 521–37.

Parenti, M. (1967). "Ethnic Politics and the Persistence of Ethnic Identification." *American Political Science Review* 61: 717–26.

Parsons, T. (1975). "Some Theoretical Considerations on the Nature and Trends of Change of Ethnicity." In Glazer and Moynihan. (eds.). *Ethnicity: Theory and Experience.* Cambridge, MA: Harvard.

Pateman, C. (1980). "The Civic Culture: A Philosophic Critique." In Almond and Verba. (eds.). *The Civic Culture Revisited.* Boston: Little, Brown.

Patterson, O. (1972). "Toward a Future that Has No Past: The Future of Blacks in The Americas." *The Public Interest* 2: 25–62.

———. (1977). *Ethnic Chauvinism: The Reactionary Impulse.* New York: Stein and Day.

Peterson, P. (1979). "Organizational Imperatives and Ideological Change: The Case of Black Power." *Urban Affairs Quarterly* 14: 465–84.

Poinsett, A. (1973). "Class Patterns in Black Politics." *Ebony,* August, 1973, pp. 36–48.

Powdermaker, H. (1939). *After Freedom: A Cultural Study of the Deep South.* New York: Viking.

Rainwater, L. (1966). "Crucible of Identity: The Negro Lower-Class Family" *Daedalus* 95: 172–216.

Ransford, E. (1977). *Race and Class in American Society.* Cambridge, MA: Schenkman.

Raspberry, W. (1989). "Another Word For Black is Despair." *Houston Chronicle,* January 6, 1989, p. 24A.

Reed, A. (1986). *The Jesse Jackson Phenomenon.* New Haven, CT: Yale.

Reed, J. (1972). *The Enduring South.* Lexington, KY: Lexington Books.

———. (1983). *Southerners: An Essay on the Social Psychology of Sectionalism.* Chapel Hill, NC: University of North Carolina Press.

Reid, J. (1981). "The Voting Behavior of Blacks." *Intercom* 9: 8–11.

Roberts, S. (1989). "Reagan's Final Rating is the Best of Any President Since World War II." *New York Times.* January 18, 1989, p. 1.

Rosenstone, S., and R. Wolfinger. (1981). *Who Votes.* New Haven, CT: Yale.

Rothman, S., and R. Lichter. (1982). *Roots of Radicalism: Jews, Christians and the Left.* New York: Oxford.

Russett, B., and D. DeLuca. (1981). "Don't Tread on Me: Public Opinion and Foreign Policy in the Eighties." *Political Science Quarterly* 96: 381–400.

Saloma, J. (1984). *Ominous Politics: The New Conservative Labyrinth*. New York: Hill & Wang.

Scammon, R., and B. Wattenberg. (1970). *The Real Majority*. New York: G. P. Putnam.

Schermerhorn, R. (1970). *Comparative Ethnic Relations: A Framework for Theory and Research*. New York: Random House.

Schiller, N. (1977). "Ethnic Groups are Made Not Born: The Haitian Immigrant and American Politics." In G. Hicks and R. Leis. (eds.). *Ethnic Encounters: Identities and Images*. North Scituate, MA: Duxbury.

Schnore, L., C. Andre, and H. Sharp. (1976). "Black Suburbanization, 1930–70." In B. Schwartz (ed.). *The Changing Face of the Suburbs*. Chicago: University of Chicago.

Schuman, H., C. Steeth, and L. Bobo. (1985). *Racial Attitudes in America: Trends and Interpretations*. Cambridge, MA: Harvard.

Schwarz, J. (1988). *America's Hidden Success: A Reassessment of Public Policy From Kennedy to Reagan*. New York: Norton.

Seeman, M. (1959). "On the Meaning of Alienation." *American Sociological Review* 24: 783–91.

Seltzer R., and R. Smith. (1985a). "Race and Civil Liberties." *Social Science Quarterly* 66: 155–62.

———. (1985b). "Race and Ideology." *Phylon* 46: 98–105.

———. (1986–87). "Race and Alienation." *New England Journal of Black Studies* 6/7: 12–28.

———. (1991). "Color Differences in the Afro-American Community and the Differences They Make." *Journal of Black Studies*. 21: 279–86.

———. (1984). "Race and Ideology: Patterns of Issue Differentiation." Paper prepared for presentation at the Annual Meeting of the National Conference of Black Political Scientists, Washington, D.C.

Shingles, R. (1981). "Black Consciousness and Political Participation." *American Political Science Review* 75: 76–91.

Slotnick, E. (1984). "The Paths to the Federal Bench: Gender, Race and Judicial Recruitment." *Judicature* 67: 371–88.

Smith, M. G. (1965). *The Plural Society of the British West Indies.* Berkeley, CA: University of California.

Smith, R. (1978). "The Changing Shape of Urban Black Politics, 1960–1970." *The Annals* 439: 16–28.

———. (1981). "Black Power and the Transformation from Protest to Politics." *Political Science Quarterly* 96: 431–43.

———. (1982). *Black Leadership: A Survey of Theory and Research.* Washington, D.C.: Howard University, Institute for Urban Affairs and Research.

———. (1984). "Black Appointed Officials: A Neglected Area of Research on Black Political Participation." *Journal of Black Studies* 14: 369–88.

———. (1984). "The Place of Liberalism in Afro-American Thought." Paper prepared for presentation at the Annual Meeting of the American Political Science Association, Washington, D.C.

———. (1988). "Sources of Urban Ethnic Politics: A Comparison of Alternative Explanations." *Research in Race and Ethnic Relations* 4: 155–87.

Sowell, T. (1984). *Civil Rights: Rhetoric and Reality.* New York: Morrow.

Spindler, G. (1977). "Change and Continuity in American Core Values: An Anthropological Perspective." In G. Direnzo (ed.). *We The People: American Character and Social Change.* Westport, CT: Greenwood.

Stuckey, S. (1987). *Slave Culture.* New York: Oxford.

Tate, K. (1986). "Explaining Black Political Heterogeneity." Paper prepared for presentation at the Annual Meeting of the American Political Science Association, Washington, D.C.

Tate, K., et al. (1988). *The 1984 National Black Election Study Sourcebook.* Ann Arbor:MI: Institute for Social Research, University of Michigan.

————. (1990). "Protest to Politics: The New Black Voter in American Elections." Paper prepared for presentation at the Conference on Representation, Reapportionment, and Minority Empowerment, Pomona College.

Taylor, R. (n.d.). "Structural Determinants of Religious Participation Among Black Americans." *Review of Religious Research*. Forthcoming.

Taylor, R., M. Thornton, and L. Chatters. (1987). "Black Americans' Perceptions of the Socio-Historical Role of the Church." *Journal of Black Studies* 18: 123–38.

Temme, L. (1975). *Occupations: Meanings and Measures*. Washington, D.C.: Bureau of Social Science Research.

Thernstrom, S. (1973). *The Other Bostonians*. Cambridge, MA: Harvard.

Thomas, M., and M. Hughes. (1986). "The Continuing Significance of Race: A Study of Race, Class, and Quality of Life in America, 1972–85" *American Sociological Review* 51:830–41.

Thompson, D. (1963). *The Negro Leadership Class*. Englewood Cliffs, NJ: Prentice-Hall.

U.S. Bureau of the Census. (1974). *The Social and Economic Status of the Black Population in the United States*. Washington, D.C.: Government Printing Office.

————. (1986). *Household Wealth and Asset Ownership, 1984*. Washington, D.C.: Government Printing Office.

————. (1983). *America's Black Population: A Statistical View*. Washington, D.C.: Government Printing Office.

U.S. Commission on Civil Rights. (1983). "Equal Opportunity in Presidential Appointments." Washington, D.C.: U.S. Commission on Civil Rights, Xeroxed.

U.S. Congress, Senate. (1972). Committee on Government Operations, *Confidence in American Institutions*. Washington, D.C.: Government Printing Office.

Van der Berghe, P. (1967). *Race and Racism: A Comparative Perspective*. New York: John Wiley.

Verba, S., and N. Nie. (1972). *Participation in America: Political Democracy and Social Equality*. New York: Harper and Row.

Walton, H. (1969). "Blacks and Conservative Political Movements." *Quarterly Review of Higher Education Among Negroes* 37:177–83.

———. (1985). *Invisible Politics: Black Political Behavior.* Albany, NY: SUNY.

———. (1988). *When the Marching Stopped: The Politics of Civil Rights Regulatory Agencies.* Albany, NY: SUNY.

Weber, M. (1946). "Class, Status and Party." In H. H. Gerth and C. W. Mills. (eds.). *From Max Weber.* New York: Oxford.

Weed, P. (1973). *The White Ethnic Movement and Ethnic Politics.* New York: Praeger.

Weiss, N. (1983). *Farewell to the Party of Lincoln: Black Politics in the Age of FDR.* Princeton, NJ: Princeton University Press.

Weissberg, R. (1986). "The Democratic Party and the Conflict Over Racial Policy." In B. Ginsberg and A. Stone (eds.). *Do Elections Matter?* New York: M. E. Sharpe.

Welch, S., and M. Combs. (1983). "Interracial Differences in Public Opinion: Issues in the 1970s." *Western Journal of Black Studies* 7: 136–41.

———. (1985). "Intraracial Differences in Attitudes Among Blacks: Class Cleavage or Consensus." *Phylon* 46: 91–97.

Welch, S., and L. Foster. (1986). "Class and Conservatism in Black America." Paper prepared for presentation at the Anual Meeting of the American Political Science Association, Washington, D.C.: D.C.

———. (n.d.) "The Impact of Economic Conditions on Voting and Policy Opinions Among Black Americans."

West, C. (1982). *Prophesy Deliverance: An Afro-American Revolutionary Christianity.* Philadelphia: West Minster Press.

Whyte, W. (1943). *Street Corner Society.* Chicago: University of Chicago.

Wiatr, J. (1980). "The Civic Culture from a Marxist Sociological Perspective." In Almond and Verba. (eds.). *The Civic Culture Revisited.* Boston: Little, Brown.

Wildavsky, A. (1987). "Choosing Preferences by Constructing Institutions: A Cultural Theory of Preference Formation." *American Political Science Review* 81: 3–21.

Williams, E. (1982). "Black Political Progress in the 1970s: The Electoral Arena." In M. Preston, L. Henderson, and P. Puryear eds. *The New Black Politics.* New York: Longman.

Williams, L., and F. Harris. (1987). "Consensus and Cleavage in Black America: Gender, Age, and Class Differences." Paper prepared for presentation at the Annual Meeting of the National Conference of Black Political Scientists, Atlanta.

Williams, W. (1982). *The State Against Blacks.* New York: New Press.

Willingham, A. (1981). "The Place of the New Black Conservatives: Groundwork for the Full Critique." Paper prepared for presentation at the Annual Meeting of the Association for the Study of Afro-American Life and History, Philadelphia.

Wilson, R. (1971). "Alienation in the Ghetto" *American Journal of Sociology* 77: 66–88.

Wilson, W. (1980). *The Declining Significance of Race.* Chicago: University of Chicago.

———. (1987). *The Truly Disadvantaged.* Chicago: University of Chicago.

Woodard, M. (1988). "The Effects of Social Class on Voluntary Association Membership Among Urban Afro-Americans." *Sociological Focus* 21: 67–80.

Wolfinger, R. (1965). "The Development and Persistence of Ethnic Voting." *American Political Science Review* 59: 896–908.

Yanley, W., E. Ericksen, and R. Juliani. (1976). "Emergent Ethnicity: A Review and Reformulation" *American Sociological Review* 41: 391–403.

Index